CHASM

CHASM

A Deep Journey

into Meaning

and Wholeness

BOB GOULET

LIONCREST
PUBLISHING

CHASM

A Deep Journey into Meaning and Wholeness

ISBN	978-1-5445-2551-8	*Hardcover*
	978-1-5445-2550-1	*Paperback*
	978-1-5445-2552-5	*Ebook*

CONTENTS

Chasm (noun): a profound difference between two situations.

Dedicated to my son, Collin.

*May you fully experience your journey, practice the art
of being fully alive, and reveal the beautiful sculpture
that lies within you.*

*Thank you for giving me the amazing gift of being
a father. My life is immensely richer with you in it.*

*I love you like only a parent can love their child:
unconditionally.*

Love, Dad

HEARTFELT APPRECIATION

Mom, as I wrote this book, I came to appreciate you so much more. To say I wasn't an easy kid would be the understatement of a lifetime. You were always there for me, especially in my darkest moments. As a father now, I deeply appreciate what it means to be there for your child. You are the model of unconditional love.

Thank you for the greatest gift and lesson in life.

Love, Bob

LOOKING INTO THE CHASM

As I OPEN MY EYES AND LOOK AT MY PHONE LAYING INNOCENTLY on the nightstand, a part of me is praying it's not morning yet. It's 4:30 a.m., July 26, 2019. *Ugh!* It's my fifty-fourth birthday today. Fifty-four...it's not supposed to be any special birthday. It doesn't end in a zero or five. You know, those birthdays that you allow yourself to make a big deal over? Yet, this birthday is a big one, the beginning of the test of my transformation.

I seldom remember my dreams, if I even have any. But last night's dream comes rushing back in high definition. It's so clear and vivid that I start to wonder if it was a dream or a memory of an actual event.

I was sitting in a trendy and crowded restaurant in the city by myself. I noticed an old girlfriend walking toward the restroom. We hadn't communicated in years. She looked young and beautiful, more beautiful than I remembered. She smiled when she looked over and saw me. The kind of genuine and deep smile that says, *Hello, it's great to see you,* and the other person instantly knows it's true. I stood up, and we walked toward each other. She was perfectly dressed. I was completely naked.

What? I am completely naked!

We embraced and had this beautiful conversation. My nakedness seemed utterly natural. Neither she nor anyone in the restaurant appeared to notice. *Huh?* We spoke of change and enlightenment, knowing that we had evolved since our fiery end. It was the kind of breakup caused by two people so laden with tragic, unhealed pasts that they can't help but let the pain dominate every relationship, especially their intimate ones. In our conversation, it was evident that we had both overcome the very pasts that derailed us. We spoke of life, lessons, and the journeys we'd taken since the last time we had yelled at each other with words we didn't really mean.

As I lay in bed, memories of the past rolled through my mind like a highlight reel. I imagine this reel plays before we die—all the memories, people, places, and experiences. I saw the beautiful, high, low, and utterly tragic moments. Seeing everything edited together, I thought, *Wow, it's been a journey. I am glad to be here. It's a miracle I am still alive.*

This book is me standing naked in a crowded restaurant, sharing my story as authentically as possible, and hopefully giving something back for all that I stole.

—Bob

INTRODUCTION

*"It is not the critic who counts; not the man who points out
how the strong man stumbles, or where the doer of deeds
could have done them better. The credit belongs to the man
who is actually in the arena, whose face is marred by dust
and sweat and blood; who strives valiantly; who errs, who
comes short again and again, because there is no effort
without error and shortcoming; but who does actually
strive to do the deeds; who knows great enthusiasms, the
great devotions; who spends himself in a worthy cause; who
at best knows, in the end, the triumph of high achievement,
and who at the worst, if he fails, at least fails while daring
greatly, so that his place shall never be with those cold and
timid souls who neither know victory nor defeat."*

—Theodore Roosevelt, 1910

SOMEWHERE DEEP INSIDE ME, SOMETHING WAS ALWAYS MISSING.
I felt a constant void and yet could never really figure out what
it was.

Was I just plain broken? Was it that I wasn't good enough? That I hadn't accomplished enough? That I wasn't loved enough? Maybe the next "thing" was going to make me feel complete. But the next thing didn't complete me. Nor did the next or the next.

The ironic part is that uneasy feeling has been my greatest motivator and source of most significant discomfort. It's led me to the depths of darkness and onto the podium and back more than once. It even took me to the edge of existence a few times and dared me to jump. My deep need to find what was missing was always there, and simultaneously, I heard another voice that told me to just give up. The friction has been both motivating and exhausting.

My journey took some wildly unexpected twists and turns. I'm glad to say that with a lot of curiosity, brutal honesty, and relentless work, I finally found what I was looking for. Ironically, it's way better than I ever imagined, yet not at all what I expected.

When I felt the calling to write this book, my sole purpose was to tell my story and possibly help or even inspire others. Maybe save some suffering. To give something back for all that I stole. You've traveled your own journey, but I hope you can see yourself at some points along mine. I decided to share my deepest moments of uncertainty in life itself: the fear, tragedy, shame, success, and transformation, to name a few. Share so that you see that it is possible. It's possible to resolve that subtle but constant ache that tells you something is missing. That life shouldn't be *this* way.

Come along on my journey. Maybe it will help you find what you have been searching for.

IN A MOMENT

THE MORNING MY ENTIRE LIFE CHANGED, I KNEW SOMETHING was different. From the moment I woke up, something felt off—really off.

My eyes were crusty, and my eyelids opened sluggishly. Everything seemed under a fog of sedation. My body was heavy and hurt everywhere. Opening my eyes took real effort. What I didn't know at the time is my subconscious was holding onto the last seconds of peace before any shred of innocence that remained in my life vanished.

I looked at the television that jutted from the wall in this unfamiliar room and saw a news reporter out on a country road somewhere, reporting on what looked like a bad wreck. They showed a car, completely smashed up and cut open. It looked something like my car. I noticed a white sheet on the ground next to the car—the kind used to cover dead bodies. The camera showed flashing lights and chalk marking different details around the crash. I could see what looked like investigators all around. It seemed like I was part of this but didn't know why.

I went to rub my face, and as I began to move my arm, it quickly stopped with the clanky sound of a heavy metal chain. It was only then that I felt a cold piece of steel around my wrist. As I moved to look, I realized I couldn't move my neck. Out of the corner of my eye, I saw what was holding my wrist: handcuffs.

An unfamiliar man's voice right next to me said, "Look who woke up." He had a noticeably sarcastic tone, one that sounded quite irritated with me.

Why is there a police officer sitting next to me, and why am I in this strange bed?

Why am I handcuffed to the bed rail?

Why can't I move my neck?

What does this news story have to do with this?

To say the whole thing was overwhelming would be an under-statement. My body felt all banged up. My neck was in a brace, and I couldn't move my head. Handcuffs restrained me to the bed, and a police officer was sitting in a chair next to me.

I'd had better mornings.

The officer said, "Look, killer, you're famous!"

I looked back at the TV, and my picture was on the screen while an investigator gave a statement. *What the hell is going on?* I asked myself.

Over the next few minutes, the officer filled me in on the details of the past few days. I learned that I had caused a horrific car crash, killed two people, and was in the hospital under police custody. The State's Attorney was about to indict me on two counts of second-degree murder.

Am I going to wake up soon? It's just a nightmare...right?

It turns out it was a nightmare but not one you ever wake up from.

The evening before had begun like many others. I recently arrived in Orlando to start Navy Nuclear Power school and went out for a few drinks with my friend Mike. We decided to go to another bar at some point, so we jumped into my car and headed on our way. As I crossed the road to enter the parking lot of our destination on the other side, I felt the impact of another vehicle. Before I could register what was happening, a woman jumped out and started screaming at me. I panicked and hit the gas, driving away from her screaming and the scene of the minor accident. It wasn't long before I realized what a stupid move that was. Mike and I agreed that this was going to be a mess for our Navy careers. So, we came up with a "brilliant" plan to ditch the car and claim it stolen. No one would ever have to know!

I was speeding along on a back road when I saw what looked like police lights behind us, approaching in the distance. Instead of taking responsibility for leaving the minor accident and pulling over, I further escalated the situation by speeding up. And that's the last thing I remember.

From accounts of the accident, I was traveling well over 100 miles an hour when I lost control of the car, struck an oncoming vehicle, and flipped multiple times. Mike was ejected from the car and died. The oncoming driver, an unsuspecting woman driving home alone, was killed on impact. I somehow survived the accident with a fractured neck and a lot of bruises and abrasions.

In a moment's time, I became the devil.

Back in the hospital bed, still handcuffed and in pain, my mother came walking into the room. I immediately saw the look on her face and the tears in her eyes, which confirmed that this was all too real. I wasn't dreaming.

It's been more than thirty years since that day, but I still remember the feelings coursing through me: disbelief, horror, massive regret, shock, pain, disappointment, and on and on. Humans are capable of so much, but this seemed like too much. In ten minutes, I went from being asleep to learning I killed two innocent people in a display of utter stupidity and irresponsibility. On top of that, I was lying in a hospital bed under police custody.

As the story of the crash, my medical condition, and the details of my criminal charges began to unfold over the next few hours, I realized my life as a twenty-year-old had changed forever. I didn't get to be sad or hurt. I was a monster in both the world's eyes and my own.

In those first few hours, I genuinely wished I'd died in the accident. I would have eagerly traded my life for those I'd just ended. At the very least, I wished I had joined them.

I stayed in the hospital for most of the week and was released from the hospital on bail. My mom had returned home to Connecticut, and a friend picked me up to take me back to the base.

He told me the military police had come to clear out all my things, and I was now living in temporary barracks. It was the place all misfits stayed while the Navy figured out what to do with unfit sailors.

In the days that followed, I hobbled around with my physical and mental wounds. Sleep was scarce, and when I did fall asleep, it wasn't long before the horror of the accident would overwhelm me. Many times, I would wake up sweating and screaming in the middle of the night. My roommates all asked to be transferred to another room, so they could sleep.

I was indicted on second-degree murder charges, leaving the scene of an accident and fleeing and eluding a police officer. It was the first time the State of Florida sought murder charges due to a vehicular death, but they said my behavior of leaving the scene of the minor accident and running from the police warranted it. At the time, second-degree murder carried a mandatory sentence of twenty-five years, so I was facing a minimum of fifty years in prison. While I'd had a couple of drinks that night, my blood alcohol level was inadmissible because I received blood in the emergency room. The State contended that the alcohol didn't contribute to the accident anyway because I needed to be cognizant for second-degree murder charges to stick.

Over the next six months, my case moved through the legal system. Finally, the state attorney and my lawyer came to a plea agreement for two counts of culpable negligence manslaughter. I accepted the plea bargain, and we prepared for sentencing. Under the Florida Sentencing Guidelines, the judge was to sentence me to seven to twelve years in prison. The Navy maintained their right to try me in military court if they deemed the civilian punishment inadequate.

My attorney hired an expert to write a proposal on alternative sentencing that presented the argument that prison had little benefit to society or me and that I was unlikely to commit another crime. It sounded great, and I was hopeful, but my attorney cautioned me to prepare for prison.

Feeling completely unprepared to be an inmate, I decided I needed to learn how to defend myself. I went to a local boxing gym and told the owner I was headed to prison. Joe, the owner, had heard of my accident and agreed to teach me some things that might help me defend myself, maybe even save my life.

A few weeks before my sentencing, I went by the gym for my last session. In the middle of the lesson, Joe grabbed my balls with his left hand and my throat with his right and drove me into the padded wall with what felt like all his strength. As I stood, pinned and stunned, he told me, "You ain't going to be the biggest or the toughest in there, and when it comes right down to it, fuck the fancy shit. Grab his balls and his throat, and find something really hard to smash his skull against until his brains are on the Goddamn ground." The lesson was duly noted, and I felt slightly more prepared for what was ahead of me. It turns out Joe's lesson was one I'd need.

My dad had been diagnosed with bladder cancer and was having his bladder removed in Boston. The court allowed me to travel to be with him during his ten-hour surgery. He came through surgery well, and after a few days of visiting, I returned to Florida for an extended stay. "The end of the line," you might say.

The base had a center for alcohol education, and they assigned me to work there once my body recovered enough. The women who worked there accepted me with open arms. We talked about all kinds of things, and before long, I began attending AA and NA. I went to a few meetings a week, got a sponsor, and worked the twelve steps.

I learned the serenity prayer and have recited it to myself almost every day since.

"God, grant me the serenity to accept the things I cannot change, the courage to change the things that I can, and the wisdom to know the difference."

I went to some tough AA meetings, and the stories of repeated struggle and absolute self-destruction stuck with me. I saw with my own eyes where my path could lead if things didn't change.

A couple of times, I seriously debated jumping bail and running off to Mexico and staying on the run for the rest of my life. One night, I called my mom and told her I was splitting, but she talked some sense into me. She convinced me to stay and do what was right. I knew I had to do my time, but a part of me really wanted to run away.

On sentencing day, I dressed in my suit and prepared myself as much as I could. My parents were both there to support me throughout the hearing. The term "dead man walking" best describes what it felt like. Once again, I knew that I would not return to life as I currently knew it. I packed the few things I had in my Navy duffle bag, realizing it was likely I wouldn't see any of this stuff soon, or ever. Prison loomed. No part of me was sure of what was to come or if I would even survive it.

We all stood as the judge entered and began my sentencing hearing. Mike's wife, the family of Karen, the woman I killed, MADD, my alternative sentencing expert, and several others spoke—as did I.

Mike's wife spoke of loss and pain. Karen's family spoke of the senseless tragedy of their loss. Her son wanted me to pay for his suffering and suggested that I never be released. While it was difficult to hear, I fully understood and imagined I would have felt similar in his situation. I would have traded my life instantly if I could bring them back, but that doesn't mean a damn thing. Nothing I could do or say could undo the pain and suffering I caused, so I sat attentively and felt their pain as much as I could. I felt the need to suffer, like I needed to carry all the pain in the room inside me. It was my burden to bear, my responsibility to feel it all.

The gravity of the situation converged in that room on that day— the crash, the tragedy, and the suffering. The suffering in everyone and my shame were my responsibility, my cross to bear. That day I began to embrace everything I stole. That day I began to embrace that every moment of my journey is my responsibility. No excuses.

A representative of MADD spoke. The state was intent on proving that alcohol wasn't the cause in charging me with second-degree murder, so it wasn't obvious to me why she was speaking. Her pain was perfectly clear. In 1985, MADD was a force to be reckoned with, and I was in no position to argue about anything.

Our alternative sentencing expert gave his report on the effectiveness of probation and rehabilitation. It was evident that there wasn't much support for this idea, even though it had a solid foundation.

The judge asked me if I had anything to say before he sentenced me. A part of me wanted to jump out the nearest window, but I stood and spoke. I acknowledged the recklessness of my actions and apologized directly to the families and to the court. I wished more than anything I could take away the pain and anguish the families felt, both for them and because that was the hardest thing for me to experience. Of course, I couldn't. It didn't feel like I could convey the depth of my regret and remorse, and even if I could have, it really wouldn't have mattered. I did what I did, and nothing I could say would change that. There would never be a chance to undo the tragedy. In that moment, I came to truly understand what total responsibility for your actions is. The perpetrator is the doer of the deed, no place for denial and blame. When I finished speaking, I sat down, feeling even more ashamed, embarrassed, and broken. In that moment, I remember thinking there wasn't much the court or anyone could do to make me feel any worse about myself and my actions. Once again, the pressure of life seemed to be pressing me beyond breaking, but breaking wasn't an option.

Human capacity is immense. When given no real choice, we either handle it, kill ourselves, or go insane. In my most intense life moments, I've forged into something stronger because there was no alternative. Having no escape required me to handle what life presented, and I did my best to do it honestly. When forging a steel blade, you repeatedly hammer the hot blade, and the metal yields and gets stronger. Hopefully, you don't shatter it in the process.

After some time, the judge ordered me to stand again. He looked at me and said a few things I don't remember, then delivered the news that sealed the next leg of my journey. He said, "I hereby sentence you to twelve years, the maximum allowable under the Florida State Guidelines and hereby remand you to the Florida Department of Corrections. Bailiffs, please remove him from my court."

I stood there frozen. A part of me had been desperately clinging to the delusion that the judge wouldn't send me to prison. No part of me had accepted that I would get twelve years; at that point, more than half of the years I'd been alive. As the bailiff opened the cuffs, I held out my hands and surrendered my freedom.

The officer led me to a small cell off the courtroom. I noticed a bare mattress and a toilet bowl. He slid the metal bars shut and told me to remove my shoelaces, belt, and tie and give them to him. "Huh?" I mumbled.

Turns out suicide in the early hours is pretty likely. They take the obvious implements to keep you from hanging yourself in the aftermath of sentencing.

Sitting in the small cell by myself, I tried to adsorb the reality of what had just happened and that I was now on suicide watch. Rational people knew that someone in my position was likely to decide that hanging themselves with shoelaces or a sheet was the best option. I kept thinking, *Twelve years? Holy shit.* I'd be lucky to be out before I was thirty. I'd be lucky to get out at all.

I sat on that bunk thinking, *What's the point of living at all?* I couldn't come up with a single reason. I mean, I had just caused the death of two people, bore witness to the immense suffering it left behind, and been deemed unworthy of the privilege of living freely in society. Cerebrally, I had a strong case for life being pointless, but something inside me knew that I must go on. I guess that's why they took everything I had; it was a shaky ledge I was teetering on.

The hours I sat in that cell were my initiation into being completely on my own. It was eerily quiet, and I was there with only me. I was now an inmate and about to enter an unknown world with no support or anyone to lean on. What remained of the little boy inside me waved goodbye.

After a few hours, guards came and transported me to Orange County Correction Center, where I was processed. They took new mug shots, fingerprints, and all the other inmate intake procedures.

I traded what remained of my street clothes for an Orange County Jail jumpsuit, and they put me in a holding cell with twenty or thirty others. It was dinner time, and I got a tray and found an empty bunk. It wasn't long before someone pointed to the television and said, "Holy shit! That's you, brother. You got real time!"

The top story on the evening news featured my sentencing, and after they showed some of the victims' families testifying, they cut to my parents, sitting hunched over, holding each other and crying together. They had just heard my sentence read, and the bailiffs were leading me away. If I thought I'd hit rock bottom before, this was an entirely new depth of my personal hell. I had never seen anything like it. I had completely broken my parents. I didn't think I could sink much lower, but that helped me find new depths of darkness.

I was in the county jail for a week or so while I waited for transport to the Florida Department of Corrections. People came and went, but I just waited. In retrospect, County Jail is a joke. I would eat my three meals, lay on my bed, and watch soap operas.

One afternoon, a guard told me that the Florida Department of Corrections would be picking me up in the morning. I didn't sleep that night, or much for the next few months, or years. I laid in my bunk thinking about what prison would be like and how I would fare. At that point, I had no idea what to expect and imagined the worst.

In the morning, I was led to a holding cell and told to change into another jumpsuit. After I put it on, the guards began the process of constraining a human who needs to be removed from society. I was chained at the waist and cuffed to the chains with shackles around my ankles. When the process was over, I completely understood what a caged animal feels like with nowhere to go and no hope for escape. My complete lack of physical control included my total mental submission—all hope lost.

At some point, guards came to get me, and I became a ward of the Florida Department of Corrections. I was led to a seat on the bus and handcuffed to the seat. We began the long ride, only stopping to pick up others also destined for prison.

You have probably never noticed the Department of Corrections buses on the highway, but now, I notice them all. They are often BlueBird buses with expanded metal sheets welded inside the windows. Inside sit the people bound to serve their time. In the front, there is a driver and a guard with a shotgun.

With my five days served in the hospital and ten days in county jail, I was down to 4,364 days and a wake-up before I'd be free to walk down the street on my own again.

2

INTO THIS WORLD, WE'RE THROWN

I STOOD IN A SMALL HALLWAY WITH TEARS RUNNING DOWN MY face, my body stinging from being pushed around. I couldn't hear anything. My head throbbed after slamming into the door frame, which was making it harder to concentrate. I knew he was screaming something, but I couldn't understand a word. My shame was overwhelming, and for the first time in my very young life, I just wanted to die. I wished someone or something would make it all stop. But it didn't.

I was six years old, standing in the hallway of our small house on Beech Road in Bloomfield, Connecticut. It was the early morning of a school day, and things had gone really wrong.

Mom had already left for work, and Dad was using our one bathroom. I really had to go, but I already knew that you don't bother Dad when he is in the bathroom. Unfortunately, I couldn't hold it anymore. I knocked on the door and said I really had to use the bathroom. He yelled out that he was busy and to wait.

A few minutes went by, and I knocked again and got the same reply, just a little louder and more agitated.

I waited until I lost the fight with my bowels and pooped in my pants. I knew this wasn't going to be good. It wasn't.

When he finally came out, the smell was obvious, as was the look on my face. He erupted! At 6′6″ and 275 lb. or so, my giant of a father exploded. He began to scream at me, insults and obscenities pouring out of his mouth. His anger continued to escalate until he shoved me hard, and I fell backward. My head smacked into the bedroom door frame, and the pain was instant. He went on about how I was a little baby because I couldn't hold my poop. In my little body and young mind, it was overwhelming. He was so mad, I literally thought he might kill me. At one point, during his rageful rant, he grabbed my arm and yanked me up from the floor. I was crying, which, of course, was met with the standard phrase I would come to know well: "Stop crying, or I'll smack those fucking tears off your face!" He made good on that promise, but my stinging cheeks only multiplied my tears. I am not sure how long this lasted, but it felt like an eternity.

When the school bus drove by the house, he lost it again. Now, he would have to take me to school, and he let me know how inconvenient this would be. At some point, he calmed down enough to tell me to clean my "diaper" and get ready to go to school.

On the way to school, he dropped the real bomb. He said he was going to come in with me and tell my kindergarten class that I was a "poopy boy." That I was late to school because I wasn't potty trained yet. He said it multiple times, and as we pulled into the school, I actually wanted to die. I was shaking, sweating, and a mess. He walked into school with me, and we went to the front office to excuse my tardiness. The woman behind the counter looked at me, and with what seemed like sympathy or concern in her voice, told me to go on to class. My father took his cue from her and left. To my relief, he didn't go through with his threat of coming to my class and exposing me.

I spent the rest of the school day in my own world. I didn't want to be in school, and I surely didn't want to go home. If I had been older, I probably never would have gone home. Every few minutes, I would touch the bruises on the back of my head, my body, and my face to see if it really happened. Unfortunately, they were real, and it did. As the clock ticked on, I got more terrified at the thought of going home.

When I got home that afternoon, my father was already there, still fired up about the morning's events. He immediately started in on me, saying he did me a favor by not coming to class. I knew that the woman at the counter hadn't really left him that choice. He told me, "If you tell your mother, you'll regret it," and I knew he meant it. I already knew that what happened between my dad and me stayed between us, which would remain the case throughout my childhood regardless of what he did to me.

My early years were dominated by a father who had his own issues. From time to time, his inability to cope with his own situation resulted in him taking it out on me. My response was most often to ask myself, *Why doesn't he love me?* Even more damaging: *What's wrong with me?*

I didn't have anyone to talk to about this, so, like many boys from my generation, I just internalized it and moved on. That was the lesson that was drilled and sometimes beaten into us. *Be a "man" and shut up.* It wasn't long before I learned to escape into any- and everything that would keep me away from the noise inside my head, and I did so early and often.

That incident happened fifty years ago, and I still remember it like it happened yesterday. At that moment, a part of my exis- tence, my youth, my innocence, and my trust in people was stolen. *If I can't trust my own father, then who can I trust? Not him, and especially not myself.*

Thankfully, my mom was able to provide some stability and bright spots throughout my childhood. Not long after the bath- room incident, Mom and I visited her side of my family in Austria, one of a handful of trips I took as a kid. Our family predominately lived in a small country town that was quiet and scenic, exactly like you might imagine Austria, and I loved being there. There was a strong sense of family, and my grandmother, aunts, uncles, and cousins always treated me well. During those trips, my uncles taught me to fish, find mushrooms in the woods, and enjoy the outdoors. One of my cousins spoke English well and helped me learn some German; she was my "big sister." We always stayed with my grandmother, a strong woman who worked hard rais- ing kids, tending to her garden, and cooking meals. The thing I greatly appreciated about my grandmother was her work ethic and responsibility. She got up every morning and put in the work: garden, animals, and meals. I truly appreciated it, and I saw it in my mom. *You get up and get after it. No excuses.*

While I stayed with my grandmother, my chore was to walk up to the dairy farmer with two milk cans and bring back milk every other day. She warmed the milk on the wood-fired stove in the kitchen and ate the fat layer that formed on the top while smil- ing at me. If you wanted eggs for breakfast, you went out in the yard, found where the chickens had laid your breakfast, and then brought them in for cooking. I didn't think much of it back then, but I appreciated the simplicity and wholesomeness of it all. It was a very different experience than life in Connecticut.

On our return from this trip, my dad picked us up from the airport. While we were away, he bought this metallic blue 1972 Pontiac Lemans convertible, and I remember the ride home with the top down. At seven, this was the coolest thing I could imagine. But when we arrived home, the entire mood shifted. I was immediately sent to my room, and then the fighting between my parents began. I wasn't sure what was going on, but it was big. After a few slammed doors, I heard my dad's car roar off, and my mom came into my room. She said, "Dad doesn't live here anymore. He left us."

Turns out, my dad was having an affair with his secretary and moved in with her while we were gone. So, now it was just my mom and me. Sometime that fall, I visited the apartment where my dad was living. I also met his girlfriend on that visit, but I don't remember much about the entire day, except I didn't want anything to do with the woman who stole my dad.

In 1972, separation and divorce weren't very common. It was just one more failure on my dad's part. While my dad often seemed like a monster to me, it hurt that he chose this other woman over us. I hated her and him for it. *What the hell did we do wrong? Why did he sneak out when we were gone? Buy a new car?*

That winter, I remember him stopping by on Christmas Day. He brought me a big present, a nice red fire truck. I opened it, but I wasn't excited for it the way every seven-year-old boy at that time would have been. I just wanted my dad. I wanted Christmas. I wanted a family. I wanted him to love me. He didn't stay long, and the fire truck...well, it never got much attention either.

The following year, my father's relationship fell apart. He ended up losing his job after he tried to fire his secretary and now ex-girlfriend. His boss told him to leave if he couldn't handle it. Shortly after his career fell apart, he had a nervous breakdown. At some point, my parents reconciled, and Dad moved back in. While a part of me was glad he returned, we never shared much of a father-son relationship.

Dad was seeing a psychiatrist for his breakdown. In my young mind, this looked like total bullshit. I had seen him do a bunch of really stupid stuff, and then, when it blew up in his face, he couldn't handle it. Instead of being accountable, he told everyone he had a nervous breakdown. It all seemed like a giant cop-out, and I grew to despise people who decided to just check out as soon as they screwed up. I wanted to do the same, but that wasn't an option for me.

His temper would flare up with me most often when Mom wasn't around. It's almost comical that a 6'6" giant of a man had to flex his muscles on his little kid. The physical stuff didn't bother me as much as the consistent distance and lack of acceptance. The biggest thing I remember is that he often told me how impressive he was and never had much good to say about me. I didn't see an impressive man, but he was an expert at making me feel like a piece of crap. Whatever I did, he would tell me about how he did it better. He was truly a legend in his own mind and left me feeling like I couldn't do anything right.

My mom was the foundation in our house. While my dad never kept a job for more than two years, my mom spent her entire career at one company. She cooked the meals, cleaned the house, and was my rock. Often overprotecting me from an unstable father, she was my angel. Dad always had an excuse. Mom just got things done. At an early age, it was clear which model I wanted to emulate.

By the time I was eleven, Mom was moving up in her career. Her job allowed us to move out of Bloomfield and into South Windsor. Life there, compared to the neighborhoods of my earlier years, was good. We would go skiing in the winter and had a small boat we hung out on in the summer. It seemed like things relaxed a bit, and I enjoyed the more frequent tranquility.

I started seventh grade in South Windsor and couldn't have felt more out of place. Already an insecure mess, I was now the kid from the other side of the tracks and didn't feel like I belonged. We weren't rich or anything, but South Windsor was a predominately white, middle-class town, and where we had lived in Bloomfield was definitely the other side of the tracks. It seemed like everyone on our street worked for one of the insurance companies or big manufacturing companies. I felt like I didn't belong there, or maybe I felt like I just didn't belong.

Dad remained a heavy drinker. He escaped his latest woe with a drink, or six, and celebrated mild success with seven. He was pretty unpredictable when he drank, and I learned to stay away when he got to that point. As a kid, I'd play with Legos or Erector sets. As I got older, I turned to records and cars—anything that could distract me from my current circumstances.

I always wanted to work. At an early age, I had a paper route. On Sunday, my sack of Hartford Courants would be bigger than me. On Thursday nights, I remember having to go door to door to collect the money for papers. By my fourteenth summer, I worked in the tobacco fields picking tobacco. A bus would pick me up at the bottom of our street early in the morning and drop me off in the evening for $2.25 per hour. I would come home so dirty every evening that I had to drop my clothes in the garage before entering the house.

My folks told me that if I wanted a car when I was sixteen, I would have to buy it myself. So, I worked as much as possible and saved almost every penny. A car represented some level of freedom, of escape.

Looking back, I can recognize that the idea of escape was always present in my life as a kid. *Eat well during the week but binge on the weekend. Drink away a bad day. Get away for the weekend. Blame it on someone else.* It seemed like we were always running away from the everyday, and I guess we all were. It wasn't that we had a bad life; I guess we were all just looking for or running from that missing piece.

By fourteen, I was grabbing for more focused escapes pretty often. I started drinking and smoking pot regularly. At the time, the drinking age was eighteen, and I looked old enough, so I became a regular at a local package store. On Fridays, I would ride my bike, hide it around back, and buy a pint. The older man that owned the place would ask how the week was, and I would comment about how it's just a job or tell him that I needed a second one after an especially hard week. While I may have started early, escape through alcohol and drugs seemed like a normal right of passage.

That was also the year I got arrested for the first time. I decided to shoplift a fishing lure from the store while my mother was shopping at the mall. I took the first one and got out of the store without detection. It was so easy I went back a few more times. It turned out to be one too many because the security guard stopped me on my way out. Stealing one fishing lure might not have been a big deal, but he made me empty my bag, and I looked like a professional shoplifter.

I met a guy named EJ at the marina where we had our boat, and he became my cool, tough "uncle." He was a Vietnam vet, had tattoos, and drank Crown Royal. He was this big game hunter and fisherman, and he taught me how to catch big fish in the Atlantic. I became a regular at the marina and often went out fishing on different boats. I loved being one of the guys on Montauk shark, bluefin tuna, and other fishing trips. While I was still a kid, these guys treated me well and let me play a big boy game. That was a great place to be.

The outdoors appealed to me. I went to a few wilderness summer camps. When I was fifteen, my folks let me go backpacking with a group in the White Mountains of New Hampshire for a few weeks, and I loved being outdoors and with adults. I had a Greyhound bus ticket home but decided to hitchhike from New Hampshire home to Connecticut on my own. It was certainly a different time.

I bought my first car at fifteen, a 1973 Camaro. It was my prized possession. I had worked hard for it and loved what it represented for me: freedom.

After being introduced to it in the marina parking lot at age sixteen, cocaine quickly became my drug of choice. *Go faster, do more, and be alert!* I felt more like myself high on cocaine than I did without. Drugs seemed to be all around me, and I was always open to trying a new high if for no other reason than to fit in. So, later that same year, I shot heroin with some friends. It was a really bad trip, and I woke up in a bed full of my own vomit on New Year's Day. I never did that shit again and stayed away from the "hard" drugs.

I never much cared about school. I preferred working on cars and making money. At sixteen, I started my own body shop in our garage and spent all my time working on cars, fishing, or skiing. I had some good friends, and when we weren't working on cars together, we were planning the next party we were going to.

I still managed to graduate high school in 1983 despite my lack of interest and eighty-six unexcused absences during my senior year. I had a pad with my dad's name on the top and just started writing excuses, so I could go to work instead of class. The school finally figured it out right before graduation, and they weren't going to let me graduate, but Mom went to the school to talk it out, and I graduated.

I was accepted at the University of Rhode Island in Mechanical Engineering, and off I went to one of the top-rated party schools in the country (at that time). I majored in partying, managed to show up for the midterms and finals in most of the classes, and had a 1.7 GPA after two semesters.

My academic performance did not spark great enthusiasm on my return home, and Dad clearly didn't want to waste any more money on my "education." One day, I opened the paper to a full-page ad that said, "It's not just a job, it's an adventure!" With that, I was off to the Navy recruiting office. It seemed like the best option I had at the time. Ironically, I wasn't running to it, but running away from my dad and my current situation.

On January 3, 1985, I was on the bus from Chicago's O'Hare Airport to the Great Lakes Training Base to start basic training. When the drill instructor came down the aisle at 4:30 a.m. the next morning, banging the side of a metal garbage can, yelling for us to get the hell up, I realized the pitch my recruiter gave me might have been missing a few of the details. *What the hell did I get myself into here?* I wondered. Not surprisingly, my recruiter was arrested for dealing cocaine before I finished bootcamp.

Bootcamp wasn't too bad after the shock wore off, and it went by quickly. I went on to A School in Great Lakes and that summer transferred to Orlando to start Nuclear Power School.

It seemed like I was starting to get my act together.

3

END OF THE LINE

THE BUS RIDE TO PRISON LASTED A FEW HOURS. I LOOKED OUT the window, for the most part, soaking in every scene I could. I knew it would be years before I rode down another dull road, seeing the endless stretch of houses, cars, and the glorious simplicity of freedom. As much as I tried to escape in the rolling scenes outside my window, the reality of my situation was never too far away. With each stop, we picked up other prisoners, and the clank of chains reminded me of the gravity of my current situation.

After hours on the road, the bus slowed as we approached Florida State Prison: the end of the line. There was an arch over the road that said, "Welcome to Florida State Prison." *Cute*, I thought. The guard on the transport bus welcomed us to the home of death row and let us know that Ted Bundy was housed in the building in front of us waiting for his date with "Ol' Sparky," the knick name for the State's electric chair. I never met Ted, but I had the dubious distinction of doing time in the same prison with him while he waited for execution.

At twenty years old, I had gone from being a Navy sailor to sitting on a hard bench in a bright orange jumpsuit, confined in a rolling cage with chains and shackles weighing on my soul. I stared blankly at the double wire fence in front of me, the twenty or thirty feet between them filled with razor wire (a wire that coils back on itself if cut), 100-foot-tall guard towers every 500 feet or so with what appeared to be a trigger-happy guard. This was my new home. Adrenaline coursed through my veins, and the sheer terror, indescribable. There was also a deep feeling of acceptance that this was where I belonged.

How in the hell am I going to hang in this place? I kept asking myself.

Equally as powerful was the crushing disappointment at just how far my life had sunk. Despite feeling complete devastation, I didn't have time to wallow in any real self-pity. Life was now nothing more than a constant state of primal survival. My adrenaline spigot was wide open and would stay that way for months and, to some degree, years. I was so wired. Completely alone.

During the intake process, you get: your head shaved, your naked body sprayed down for lice, more fingerprints, mug shots, prison ID (102101), prison-made underwear, blue jeans, work shirt, and shoes. After a few hours, we were led out onto the compound for the first time.

There was, of course, a committee of degenerate assholes who welcomed us with comments like, "Nice ass, pretty boy! Can't wait to fuck you tonight!" And my favorite, "You gonna be my bitch, pretty white boy!" This was some shit right out of a movie. The young white boy goes to prison, and there is a waiting line ready to turn him into some prison sex slave. And it wasn't just the inmates. The guards taunted us too with their constant, "Welcome home, boys!" If I thought I was tapped out on adrenaline, each new thing I saw proved that there was always more. My fear, mixed with the adrenaline, created an urge to start fighting right now. I figured, *Why wait until later? Let's just get on with it.*

The prison system was so crowded that we went to the annex where they had built wooden barracks to house the overflow of new arrivals. I was assigned a bunk in a room with a hundred or so bunks and told to drop my stuff and come up for my briefing. It was nothing more than the basics on rules and clarity on anything that could get us in more trouble.

That was that. I was now home, with nothing to do except figure out how to survive.

The obvious conversations started up with other inmates. "What are you in for?" and "How long have you got?" My twelve years wasn't much in this crowd since many of the guys had multiple life sentences and mandatory quarters requiring them to do twenty-five years with no chance for early release. Since I was only twenty and had twelve years, I was considered a high-risk by the state and thrown into maximum-security and remained there for my entire sentence.

I wandered out on the yard for the first time, and the racial divide became obvious right away. For the most part, whites hung with whites, blacks with blacks, and hispanics the same. In writing this book, I considered skipping the racial conversation, but it wouldn't be authentic to avoid it.

When you walk into the gates of prison, you are immediately faced with 1,000 individual threats, and you have to quickly sort that shit out, or you'll drive yourself insane. It was immediately obvious how the first sorting pass was done. *You are the same race as me, or not.* It was immediate and simple. It seemed pretty obvious that human evolution wired us to be able to make quick decisions on friend or foe, lest we get eaten by the saber tooth tiger. In my early days in prison, everyone looked like a saber tooth tiger.

In the Florida Department of Corrections in 1985, there were three distinct segregations: whites, blacks, and hispanics. At the lowest operating level, especially when tensions rose, we were "crackers," "niggers," and "spics" and referred to each other as such. As a Connecticut-raised "liberal" boy, this blew me away. There were different levels of interactions in prison, but at the core, especially when tensions rose, you belonged to the group of people that shared your skin color. In every group, there were people of wildly different backgrounds, geographic and socio-economic. It wasn't that we came from the same place, committed similar crimes, or liked the same stuff—it was only that we shared the same color skin. That was all that we needed to determine our group. There were some gang affiliations, but they followed the racial divide as well.

The white guys looked mostly like a dysfunctional biker gang with a few creepy guys thrown in. I wandered toward my "assigned" group, clearly not looking like a biker gang guy and hopefully not one of the creepy ones either. There was no welcoming committee, but it was someplace to hang out that felt safer than standing in the middle of the dirt lot waiting for some shit to happen. When you put a lot of dysfunctional guys together in a cage, it's just a matter of time before some shit starts. Finding a tribe to belong to appeared to be a required survival move.

Before long, one of the biker dudes asked me the basics and if this was my first stint, which of course, he already knew the answer to. Others joined in, and I got the rundown of who had killed whom or gotten "setup" in some drug bust. I learned the hierarchy of crimes between inmates. In the joint, there is no worse crime than child molestation. If there is one universal truth everyone agreed on, it's that child molesters are the scum of the earth, with rapists a close second. The older guys told me who to look out for, who to avoid, and any other important information for my survival over the next twelve years. Most of the guys were quick to tell me I got screwed and didn't belong in this shithole. I played as low-key as I could manage, and that seemed to work pretty well.

One of my first questions was, "What's with the 'boys' who are obviously trying to be girls?" In a population where 98 percent of the guys were projecting some attempt at being masculine, these guys were doing everything they could to project being feminine. It was explained that the "sissies" were a group of "boys" who did everything they could to look and act like women. They were the "fuck boys" of the penitentiary and worked hard with the limited resources they had to let you know. In prison, the drag queen show is for real. All the "sissies" are basically sex slaves, owned by their "daddy," and you dare not touch one without "daddy's" permission. *Got it; no issue there.* There was the further explanation of the boys who were still trying to act tough but had given up—"closet fuck boys," as they were known. A number of them were pointed out. These were the boys, mostly late teens, early twenties who had been broken sexually and now used by their "daddy" in "secret." I guess they were still "protesting" their use as a prison sex slave and weren't ready to fully embrace it as the "sissies" had.

A few of the blunter guys asked me if a twenty-year-old white boy that didn't even commit a "real" crime was going to stand up or "bitch" up and become owned by someone else. I was going to be tested for sure, I was told. *Awesome!* There were a few guys already talking about how they were looking to "break me in." This knowledge does not help you sleep any better at night, I can assure you.

Once in a while, I would find myself confronted by someone who clearly wanted to test my will to remain celibate in prison, but the open nature of the annex and tribal protection kept those encounters pretty mild. There was always a piece of me that was scared shitless and didn't feel very tough, but I must have faked it well enough for most of the "daddies" looking for their next lover to move on to easier targets.

In the years since getting out, I often hear people talk about how we humans no longer have any use for the fight-or-flight wiring within us. They clearly haven't been sitting on the bus waiting for the gate to open to a maximum-security prison or standing in the prison yard when someone wants to break your very soul and turn you into their bitch. It's as primal as being on the open plain with a saber tooth tiger bearing down on you.

My mom came to visit me a few weeks after I arrived. She was a bit late that morning but very collected, and I tried to be as well. I was a fucking mess but didn't want her to worry any more than she already had. The constant tension, crappy food, and lack of sleep were wearing on me, but I tried to hide it as much as possible while we sat together. After I got out, she told me that she sat at the gate for thirty minutes, crying at the sheer magnitude of it all. Seeing the gates, razor wire, gun towers, and death row were just too much. She knew she couldn't show me, so she collected herself before coming inside to visit. The guilt of killing two people weighed heavily on my mind, but it was knowing the magnitude of stress I put on my mom that was often the hardest.

Visitation in prison is an ordeal for both sides. For inmates, there's always a full body search going in and coming out. In maximum-security, that means stripping down, lifting your arms, turning, lifting your penis and balls, turning around again, bending over, and spreading your asshole wide open to make sure you aren't smuggling things in or out. There were never any exceptions to this rule. It could be pretty intimate on the visitor side as well.

One thing you lose quickly in prison is any semblance of privacy. In the annex, there were open bathrooms, the sit-down toilets had a very low wall, and you crapped and, for many, masturbated in the open. Nothing like walking into the bathroom, and half of the guys have some old porno magazine in one hand while they take care of their business in the other. The whole thing desensitizes you pretty quickly. The first few times I saw one of the "sissies" performing orally or getting it in the ass was also shocking. But I quickly adapted to the entire circus. It's pretty crazy what you become accustomed or numb to.

In April and May of 1986, there were three executions at FSP while I was there. The lights dimmed and seemed to flicker, and you could hear the prison's generator running. There were all kinds of rumors as to why this happened. Most people believed they used the generator to power Ol' Sparky so that the local power company could not be tied to the execution. It was a really creepy time, being on the grounds when they put someone to death. It touched something primal in me as it was a bit close to home from where I was standing. Today, when I hear people talk about the death penalty, I go back to those nights.

After some months of sitting around wasting the days, talking shit, and being bored out of my mind, they told me I was being transferred to Lake Correctional Institution (LCI), another maximum-security prison closer to Orlando. On transfer day, I got all suited up, shackled up, and took another bus ride. By this point, I was used to chains and shackles, full cavity searches, and being treated like a wild animal that could erupt at any second.

> Submission (noun): the action or fact of accepting or yielding to a superior force or to the will or authority of another person.

Being chained, cuffed, and shackled was an experience of full physical and mental submission for me. Having grown up with a very dominant father, I had learned to fully submit mentally yet usually had some semblance of physical freedom. At least I had the option to run. With the bright orange jumpsuit, chains, cuffs, shackles, and surrounding guards and firearms, I submitted completely. Prison isn't some game or role-play situation; there is no "safe" word. I lost *all* control, including over my physical body. It felt like being a wild animal stripped of all freedom when it was meant to run.

There is a profound difference between mental and physical submission. While total physical submission is a pure loss of physical freedom, mental submission is more complex and deceptive. When the chains and shackles were removed, I was free to move freely, but that didn't free my mind. Only I could do that.

The question of why a circus elephant doesn't run away from the flimsy chain and post they are attached to is often explained as they develop the belief that they can't. When they are young, they are chained to a post and physically can't break free. Eventually, this leads to them believing it's not possible, and their mental submission typically lasts a lifetime. Having lived in the confines of maximum-security prisons and been chained and shackled numerous times, I totally get how that submission could become permanent.

My most profound learning in prison was the separation of physical and mental submission. True internal freedom is irrelevant to external freedom. In fact, I doubt I could truly experience complete internal freedom having not experienced total submission. When I stand on a mountain top or the beach at sunrise with a view that goes on forever, I often acknowledge the chasm between that experience and full submission. While I'm not recommending a stint in prison, I do believe that some of the harshest situations provide the opportunity to experience perspectives that cannot be realized without having gone through them. I also believe that our mental submission is an epidemic in the world today.

My introduction to LCI was similar to FSP. As I walked onto the yard, I was met with catcalls and promises of "love" tonight. I started off in a dorm because there were just too many people. It was something like 150 inmates in a big room with two-high bunks around the walls and single-high bunks in the middle of the room so that the guards had a better view, with a large bathroom and caged shower that was open certain hours in the day.

In researching for this book, I was surprised to learn that the United States is the world leader in mass incarceration. In 2021, the United States had 2.1 million people incarcerated, about 0.7 percent of our entire population. This equates to about 25 percent of the world's total detainees, yet the U.S. has only about 4.5 percent of the world's population. We incarcerate 639 people per 100,000. According to the Institute for Criminal Policy Research, this compares with a world median of 145, 107 for Canada, and 69 for Germany. Not exactly consistent with the "land of the free." Having read the alternative sentencing plan our expert prepared, I wonder how we got to be the country with the highest incarceration rate of any country in the world. My instinct tells me that we gravitate to "simple" solutions for complex problems. "Lock the convicts up" is an easy out to a complex problem.

Everyone at LCI had real time, and my twelve years was one of the shortest sentences. There were plenty of people with multiple life sentences or natural life. Natural life means you get out when the hearse comes to get you.

The yard was something out of a movie: a few tired basketball courts, tin roof, open weight "room," and dirt track to walk or run on. We had a big mess hall, a building with some classrooms, and a chapel. There was a small commissary with one window, where cigarettes, toiletry items, a few snacks were sold and another window, where you dropped off and picked up your laundry. There was a small retention pond in the middle of the yard, as is common in Florida.

I don't remember if working was required or not, but I elected to go to work in the kitchen. I needed something to do and figured I could learn to cook, maybe eat a little better, and stay out of trouble. There were several experienced cooks and chefs in the kitchen, all inmates, and I quickly started to learn how to cook for 700 inmates. My teachers had all been cooks or chefs on the outside and were all doing long stints or life for murder, rape, or drugs. Once the guards realized I would work hard and not cause any problems, they treated me well, and the kitchen, for the most part, was pretty laid back. You did have to sign out the knives and things, but we never had any incidents.

It wasn't long before I was "allowed" to smuggle some food out of the kitchen after each meal to sell to my regular customers as a reward from the guards for taking care of my job and not causing any trouble. This gave me a little money to buy something from the commissary from time to time and was a right of passage. It also helped me fit in. It's interesting that no matter where I have ended up in life, there has always been a way to work with the system in place.

One Sunday night, a few months after I was at LCI, I went into the shower just before closing to clean up after my shift in the kitchen. Taking a shower in the cage is like a big high school gym shower, except there is a large metal gated door to keep everyone out when it's closed. Plus, this is a maximum-security prison, so you need to be alert all the time. I was really tired that night and not paying attention.

The cage was pretty empty. As I stood under the hot water with my eyes closed, I heard the hard metal clank of the gate close. A rush of primal fear ran through my body. I immediately knew this wasn't good and hoped it didn't have anything to do with me. I took a deep breath, slowly opened my eyes, and looked around. Tiny, one of the biggest Black guys in the population and known "daddy," was showering a few showerheads down from me and looking right at me. He had made sexual comments to me before, so it was no shock to see him standing there. I saw a few of his buddies at the gate standing guard. One of them sneered, "Time for lovin', cracker." I quickly put the situation together and knew that I had just fucked up and put myself in a position that would fully test my will to remain a prison virgin. About that time, he stared right at me and said, "Suck my dick, cracker."

FUCK! I said to myself. I quickly ran about a million options through my mind and decided to ignore him and keep showering. Before long, he was standing next to me and poked my shoulder hard. He had a disturbing erection and a smile on his face. "I said, 'Suck my dick, cracker'!" he said with a more agitated voice.

Tiny seemed about twice my size, and me standing there butt-ass naked didn't bolster my confidence one bit. My final lesson with Joe came to mind. "When shit gets real, grab his balls and throat and find something really hard to smash his head into," flashed in my head.

I took a deep breath and committed every ounce of my being as I turned to square up with him. I looked him in the eyes as I reached down and grabbed his balls like my life depended on it, as it probably did. I squeezed like I was going to rip them off his body and quickly reached up and grabbed his throat with the other hand and tried to tear his Adam's apple out of his throat. I used every ounce of adrenaline coursing through my body to drive his head into the concrete wall just behind him. He wasn't expecting this, and when his head hit the wall, there was a wicked thud. I continued looking at him, eye to eye. I repeatedly drove his head into the wall before his body began to buckle. There was blood everywhere. Out of nowhere, one of his buddies tackled me. Tiny dropped to the floor, and his buddy began kicking me in the body and face. After some time, the guards came running in with their clubs, and the "party" was over.

We were both covered in blood, and the guards told me to wash up. Tiny was quickly taken out to the infirmary. I was escorted to my bunk to get some clothes on. There was clapping, cheers, and taunts from the other inmates, but I didn't pay much attention. One of my eyes had swollen shut, and my lower lip was split open, but other than that, I was fine.

After the infirmary, they took me to an office for interrogation. The guards weren't stupid, but after a few attempts of getting me to talk, they realized I wasn't going to say anything and knew I wasn't the propagator in this thing. If there is one supreme rule in the joint, it's don't snitch, no matter what. I spent the night in an isolation cell and had the same conversation with the warden in the morning. He threatened to send me to "jit" school at Sumter Correctional, which, at the time, had a reputation for being the young inmate gladiator school. He told me he was sending me to the prison psychologist for evaluation.

Back on the yard, racial tension was elevated for a while, and I waited for something else to come from it, but the whole thing just faded, and I went back to my daily routine. I'm pretty sure there was stuff going on behind the scenes that I wasn't aware of that kept things calm.

For much of the population, this was a racial incident. For me, Tiny was an asshole that wanted to violate me, and I didn't want to be violated. While my time in prison gave me a deep experience in the ease and, at times, the necessity to separate myself by race for my own safety, it didn't change my core belief that we are all just human. There are amazing people of all types, and there are assholes as well. Often, I think we confuse the two ideas.

I never saw Tiny again. He was transferred out from the infirmary. While the whole thing sucked, it did earn me a tough or insane reputation that helped me avoid any further major conflict during my stint at LCI. Everyone knew that I wasn't backing down, and that made doing time a whole lot easier.

Jan was the prison psychiatrist, and we met shortly after the shower melee. Jan was a young guy with long hair who seemed like a hippie intent on doing something meaningful. He was definitely interested in helping, and we developed a great working relationship. I met with him almost every week of my stint at LCI, and we talked about all kinds of things. It was great to have someone to talk to about prison life that wasn't an inmate. My impression of him was that he sincerely wanted to help me, and his low-key approach helped me open up to counseling. The gravity of my situation greatly contributed to my opening as well.

I was clearly tense, and after our second session, he asked if I wanted to try some relaxation tapes. As someone always open to new experiences, I figured this positive one was worth a shot. I went into this quiet little room with the Radio Shack cassette player, lay down on the floor, put on the headphones, and pressed play. In prison, thirty minutes of safe, quiet peace was like gold for me. Each week, I so looked forward to those thirty minutes. My favorite was a breathing technique in which I imagined each breath pulling the tension from a part of my body and exhaling it. I was amazed at how much lighter I felt after these sessions. This became my go-to mental game all the time and was definitely the beginning of training the mind-body emotional relationship I continue to hone today. Over the next few years, I listened to everything he had but always ended up going back to this sequence.

After some time, he invited me to join his weekly group. This was a group of about a dozen inmates who came to talk about either a subject someone needed to discuss or one Jan provided. In group, I gained a much deeper understanding of human experience and the stories we tell ourselves and others. My first instinct was to judge, but as time went on and people moved in and out of the group, I began to pay more attention, listen more, and truly see into some of the darker and confused humans on Earth. I began to look into my own internal mess. It was my first experience looking at my own story and some of the faulty framework that supported it. It was the first time I began to get an even deeper appreciation that my life is my responsibility. That my human experience and expression were all mine, and blaming anyone else for any of it was just a cop-out. I didn't have some enormous revelation or transformation, but I began to shed some light on my dysfunctional human framework. I began the process of doing my deep work.

There were very few emotions displayed or discussed in the group beyond anger, frustration, and occasionally fear. The reality is, most guys in my generation didn't even consider much beyond those. We let things build up and vent with anger or escape through some form like a drink, drugs, or sex. It's what was modeled for us and what we knew. I wasn't hiding anything or missing anything because I didn't know what I didn't know. I think it's hard for many people today to understand, but that's what was modeled for us and what we knew.

My twenty-first birthday was spent behind bars. The guys in the kitchen made me a birthday cake with a naked lady decorated on the top, and I was introduced to pruno. Pruno is a prison wine, and a few of the old-timers were pretty good at making it. They mixed yeast, sugar, and orange juice with some warm water, and it turned into a concoction that tastes like a screwdriver the morning after being left outside on the picnic table on a warm evening. They would mix it up in a gallon jug, hide it in the ceiling, and put a bag over it to collect the fermentation gases so as not to be detected. The stuff would rot your gut but give you a damn good buzz. A few of the guards cared, and a few knew what was happening, so we kept it low and from time to time escaped in this swill. It definitely wasn't the twenty-first birthday I imagined, but the guys made it okay. I appreciated them for that. "Maybe you can celebrate thirty in the free world," one of my buddies toasted. *Hopefully*, I thought. He is still serving out his natural life sentence today.

In the kitchen, one of my buddies had a "closet fuck boy" that he kept. From time to time, he would let me know they would be in the flour storage room and to keep an eye out. When "The Man" came around, I would drop something big and metal to alert. Anytime I needed a bag of flour or sugar out of the room, I'd keep an eye out for "unknown" stains on the bags. As time went on, he would offer up his "boy" for services to me. While I appreciated being included, I passed and am glad to say I remained a prison virgin for my entire bit. It fascinated me how some guys were willing to trade being used as a sexual slave for protection from the rest of the population. It opened my eyes to the cop-outs and tradeoffs I make in my own life and where my boundaries are. For me selling out wasn't an option I considered.

We had a riot one night, and I watched this young guy get his head smashed in with the metal wringer from a mop bucket about twenty feet from me. It was one of the most gruesome things I have ever witnessed firsthand. They had to rush him to the emergency room, and he never returned. I stayed in my bed during the whole thing and watched the raw brutality of humanity. The typical racial divides and slurs were flying, and so was the blood, all red from what I could tell. The riot squad came in after a while, and after a few more heads got cracked open with batons, it was over. The racial tension on the yard was so thick you couldn't cut through it for a while, and it took months to subside to its normal operating level.

In the mid- '80s, there was still some idea that prison could be rehabilitative, and inmates were allowed Pell Grants. A "strip mall" school out of Ft. Lauderdale taught an Associate's Degree in small business that we could attend at night for the cost of the Pell Grant. I signed up and spent four nights a week in class learning about starting a business. I was now a convicted felon and told I probably couldn't get a job when I got out. The concept of Bob's Body Shop was created, and the class culminated with a full business plan. I still have the copy that was printed on an early dot-matrix printer on my bookshelf to remind me where I came from.

As I settled into the daily routine of prison life, working in the kitchen, going to counseling, and attending school, I started working on my health. We were allowed to run on a dirt track that circled the yard, mostly along the fence and guard towers. My favorite running partner was a Black guy named Billy, and we became known as "salt and pepper running" to most of the population, which we both had fun with as neither of us bought into the racial lines that dominated the prison yard (unless we had to, for our own safety). After about a year, we were running twenty to thirty miles a week.

Just like in any good prison movie, I started lifting weights as well. Our weight "room" was a dirt patch in the middle of the yard covered by a tin roof. You want to get strong fast, get out on the iron in the joint. I worked out with my kitchen group mostly, and we worked out in the afternoon when it was often steamy hot. When I was released, I was lifting a couple of hours a day, running six days a week and in great shape.

Working out was part building a body to defend myself and part putting on a show that I had the heart to do whatever it took. In prison, a white boy in his early twenties is always being sized up to be broken, and showing intense tolerance for training and pain helped send the assholes on to easier prey. I've been to plenty of gyms in the free world since then and often have a little laugh at all the strutting going around in the fancy air-conditioned gym with sanitizing wipes and headphones. It's a far cry from working out on the yard, under a tin roof in the middle of a hot summer day in central Florida with a bunch of convicts to keep you real.

It didn't occur to me at the time, but I felt and thought better when I was working out and eating to build muscle. At the time, it was about being part of the crew, putting on a show, and building muscle as a sign of strength. Consistently pushing to lift a new personal record was something to feel good about as well.

Prison life is pretty simple. Don't show weakness, and make sure you step up when challenged. Not much noise. Any sign of emotional weakness invites intrusion from someone else. My childhood had taught me to keep my "weaker" emotions to myself, which served me well in prison. It's not that I didn't feel fear, anxiety, and depression; I just did all I could to keep it to myself. "Fuck that" or "Fuck you" was the depth of my emotional response.

Christmas was definitely the worst of the holidays for me. On Christmas Eve, we all sat on our bunks while the guards passed out some candy in plastic coffee cups from the Salvation Army. I remember sitting on my bunk, looking at what they gave us and whatever small amount of genuine enthusiasm I felt drained right out of me. I know, it was nice that anyone did anything for us convicts on Christmas, but that cup was a giant reminder of how low my life had sunk. I always gave it away to someone that seemed to enjoy it because I didn't.

We usually had turkeys on Christmas, and we tried to make a special meal for the population. I was rarely on the kitchen's dining hall side, and I imagine that by the time we cut it all up and slopped it onto an old, banged-up metal tray, many inmates had the same feeling about dinner.

Prison is a microcosm of existence itself. The methods we employ to deal with our human predicament just seemed more transparent in prison. At our simplest, we seem wired to need an enemy or enemies. We use enemies to remove some portion of the unknown population around us from our consideration. Beyond our evolutionary wiring, it seems to me that our need for certainty drives this, using labels and enemies to create a false sense of certainty. In prison, race was the primary selection criteria. Another enemy was "The Man," more specifically the prison guards. The Man was under scrutiny by all inmates and called out by many for even the most minor of seemingly innocuous moves, which I always found amusing considering we were all inmates in a maximum-security penitentiary. Talk about throwing stones from a glass house.

In my thirty years since leaving prison, I have consistently noticed the same need for enemies. Whether on the world stage or the local stage, there always seem to be groups claiming to be victims of someone's or something's perpetration. At some level, almost everyone seems to believe that someone or something is out to get them. It makes me wonder if this is just our human condition.

After the better part of a year in the dorm at LCI, I was moved into the cell block and a cell with Eddie. The cell was a bunk bed up against a wall, with a small table, sink, and toilet bowl with no seat mounted to the wall. It was maybe 6′ × 10′. Eddie was another Vietnam vet with a bunch of life sentences for a shootout with police that left a few of them dead. Eddie's body was littered with shrapnel scars from a land mine that he took the brunt of in 'Nam, and his body was a mess. He was an easy-going guy most of the time but had these crazy flashbacks. He told me that if I woke up in the night and he was on the floor speaking Vietnamese to just stay silent in my top bunk and not move. On multiple occasions, I woke up in the middle of the night to him on the floor back in 'Nam. A couple of times they found him in the pond laying in the grass back on patrol. For our years together, I always slept with one eye open. I am not sure I ever actually slept in prison.

One thing that struck me in the joint was the number of Vietnam vets that ended up in prison. The Bureau of Prison Statistics reports that in 1978, 24 percent of all prison inmates were veterans of the Vietnam War, and it seemed that way at LCI. I have the greatest respect for all of our soldiers who see combat and try and readjust to "normal" life.

Along the way, some inmates looked out for me as the "kid who didn't belong here." After the shower incident, some of Tiny's friends threatened me and said they would get that straight, but nothing ever came of it. I may have had a guardian angel or two inside the wire.

There were a few guys at LCI that were "legends." The guys who have more life sentences than you can count on both hands and a vibe that says they are the real thing when it comes to pure badass running through their veins. There are a lot of guys trying to be that, but there are few who don't have to try. They just are. David was one of those guys. Creature, as he was known, was a giant of a guy who befriended me. He had several tattoos back when tattoos were mostly the art of Vietnam vets and bikers. Creature was both. He had been one of the leaders of the Outlaw Biker Club and had a bunch of life sentences for killing rival biker guys and burying them with a payloader behind the bar, as I understood it. He was very involved in the Chapel at LCI and had this crazy tranquility about him. When I met him, he was like this teddy bear that everyone knew not to mess with. He had found something along his journey that had truly given him peace, and I felt it. He seemed to take an interest in making sure I got out in one piece. Years after I got out, my mom told me that he approached her in the visiting center and told her, "It's going to be okay, Mama; we'll make sure he's okay."

While I couldn't articulate it at the time, Creature had found peace in the midst of chaos. Not only did he live in a place of chaos, but his past surely implied a high degree of it. He was a physical giant, and I didn't have to stretch my mind far to believe he killed a bunch of guys and buried them with a payloader in an earlier life. While quite a few inmates claimed to be "saved," it often felt less than fully authentic to me. But I could feel it in Creature. To me, his vibe was amazingly centered and peaceful. He gave me an incredible gift in his example that it's clearly possible to realize internal peace regardless of the chaos you've caused, experienced, or find yourself in the middle of. When things seem tough in my life, or I get wrapped up in my own chaos, I often remind myself that if Creature could find peace, it is always available to me as well.

LCI had motion sensors in the ground between the fences, but it wasn't long before I heard that they had to turn them off during big rainstorms. On a few occasions, we had escape attempts during the nights of massive storms. We had a lockdown for count one particular time, and a friend of mine a few cells down had escaped. The sound of the bloodhounds always sent shivers up my spine. They would bark, just dying to get to work, and you could see the crew at the fence with some clothes they got from the escapee's cell to get the hounds on the scent, and off they would go. To my knowledge, they caught everyone within a few hours or days, but the primal sound of bloodhounds and their readiness to hunt for a human is still crystal clear in my memory. I definitely will never own a bloodhound.

Over my years in prison, something profoundly changed. When I got there, all I could see were gun towers, wire, and boundaries. From every angle and every place, that's all I saw and felt. It was my focus, and it was disempowering. As I settled into holding my own ground, working in the kitchen, working out, school, and counseling, I began to focus less on the "cage" I was in. By the time I left LCI, I didn't notice them anymore. It's ironic that the first time I felt true freedom in my life was in a maximum-security penitentiary surrounded by razor wires, gun towers, and bloodhounds. As I wrote this book, the structure and freedom I found in prison shocked me because it would take me decades to understand the lessons and fully realize them in the free world.

After a few years in prison, I was thriving. My body, mind, and emotions were strong, and I felt centered and at peace. It was the first time in my life that I didn't feel a strong internal friction—that feeling that something was off—or feel the need to escape.

In prison, I was practicing extreme self-care. How did that happen? For me, there was a hunger to prove I was more than my reckless actions on that tragic evening—that I was more than the chaos of my life to date. I needed to make more of myself than what the monster society had deemed me after the accident. Part of it was also that there was a lot of gain time on the line, and I wanted to make sure I got out as fast as possible, but that was just the spark. The real momentum came from the burning desire to find peace and be different than my current circumstances.

The State of Florida was sending a lot of people to prison in the '80s and wasn't building prisons fast enough. The Federal Courts forced Florida to release prisoners early every time they reached a set cap, and by 1987, that was every few weeks. The Department of Corrections (DOC) managed this by giving us gain time for each month we served with good behavior. Gain time was credit toward time served. Not long after my incarceration, they began giving two- or three-months credit for each month served with good behavior. On average, prisoners were serving 35 percent of their sentence as opposed to the 85 percent intended. For me, this was a blessing. As time went on, my behavior got even better because you could lose all your earned gain time with a single violation for bad behavior. No one ever told us where we were, in terms of time served, and when we would be released, but we constantly discussed where we thought we were.

In the spring of 1989, they told me that I was eligible to go on work release. A week later, I packed up my laundry bag, and my days in max were over. I arrived at a DOC work release center outside of Orlando in the swamps. It was like a locked-down motel with four guys in a room. We were all supposed to find jobs and try to get reacquainted with society. The hope was this experience would make the transition into the free world easier. At twenty-four, I was now a convicted felon, didn't have a penny to my name, no driver's license, no car, and everything I owned fit in a sack the size of a king-size pillowcase. But I wasn't doing time in a maximum-security prison anymore.

Scott, a family friend, got approved to check me out of work release one Saturday. We went to a large hotel across from SeaWorld in Orlando for some event hosted by a local radio station. Overwhelmed doesn't come close to what I felt. It had been years since I drove down a road, could get a soda at the convenience store, or was around people I didn't know. The whole experience shocked me in ways I wasn't prepared for.

We stopped at a 7-Eleven, and I went in to buy a soda because, well, I could. All I can say is that if you want to appreciate the simple things in life, take them completely away for a few years. The few minutes I spent in the store were beyond magical and brought tears to my eyes. I remember sitting in the car holding my soda. I didn't want to open it, afraid the moment might vanish, and I'd be back in the joint. Scott asked, "Is everything okay?" and I nodded yes, afraid my voice might crack. I opened the Coke and took a sip of freedom.

A local radio station was hosting an event in the atrium of the hotel. Scott thought I might enjoy the scenery after years locked up. All I could focus on was the crowd of people and the "threat" they represented. A couple of people bumped into me, and I had to check my immediate reaction to smack the shit out of them. I found a place near the koi pond that was isolated and, after a bit, was standing next to a chef with a tall white hat and an embroidered white chef's jacket. We started to chat, and I asked if they might be hiring. He asked about my experience, and I told him I learned to cook and bake in prison. I explained that I was on work release and needed a job. I wasn't sure if he would call security and have me removed or let me stay. Steve was totally cool; he told me he had screwed up a number of times and spent a night in jail. He gave me his card and told me to come for an interview the following Monday. If I doubted destiny, well, that moment cleared that up for me.

On Monday, I took the work release van to the hotel for my interview. I toured the kitchen, met the bakery staff and the executive chef, and talked with Steve about what I knew and didn't know about the kitchen. I also met with the head of security and HR. A few days later, to my surprise, they offered me a job as a baker. The head of security told me I had to walk a perfect line, and I did. We actually became friends, and he always seemed to be rooting for me. I never let him down and never stopped appreciating the chance they took on me.

Getting a job was awesome because I got to go to work almost every day. I worked hard and always did more than was asked— on or off the clock. The various chefs trained me in new techniques, and I started to work additional shifts in the main kitchen. We had these huge Sunday brunches, and the executive chef taught me to carve ice sculptures of dolphins and swans on the loading dock. Here I was with a chainsaw and sharp carving tools on Saturday afternoon carving three-foot-tall blocks of ice. *If only my chain gang buddies could see me now!*

The early release credits continued to come. One night I came back from work, and they informed me that my "wake up" was a few days away, and I was going to be released. I called a friend, and she said she would pick me up at 10:00 a.m. sharp.

WAKE UP

I DIDN'T SLEEP THE LAST NIGHT INCARCERATED. MY ROOMMATES and I sat around all night talking about what we would do in the free world. The next morning, I would be a free man for the first time in three and half years. At 6:00 a.m., I took a shower, packed up my stuff into my laundry bag, and waited till 10:00 a.m. The clock never moved slower. When I finished signing all the papers, I was free to go.

As the metal door slammed behind me one last time, Sandy stood out front next to her maroon 240z. There hasn't ever been a prettier site. Once again, it was just like the movie scene where the convict gets out of prison. As we drove away, the Guns and Roses song "Paradise City" played on the radio. I remember laughing to myself that the grass was greener and the girls—well, they were actually girls.

While not being incarcerated was awesome, the reality was that I was now twenty-four years old and completely starting from scratch. As a convicted felon, it felt like I had a scarlet letter on my chest. I shared the same moment with every new person I met: they learned I was a convict, and I waited for their response.

Beyond the scarlet letter, the structure I had built my life around in prison was now gone, and I was unprepared for that. I was staying with family friends, I didn't have a driver's license or car, and everything I owned in the world fit into a regular laundry bag. I had less than $1,000 to my name (what the state let me keep from my job). It wasn't prison that I missed; it was the structure and flow.

It's much easier to thrive when you're in a highly structured environment with few distractions available. In prison, I had a running track, workouts, work, school, counseling, and friends. Lights out and lockdown were at 10:00 p.m. My entire life was in one square mile. It was structured and complete. Now, I was out, and the structure of my day and life was completely mine. There were a lot of distractions and little structure.

It's really interesting looking back because I can now see the profound influence the structure of prison provided. I thought I had the pieces of a successful life figured out. As soon as I was free, I realized it wasn't solely my self-discipline that helped me thrive. The structure in prison facilitated much of my dedication. Don't get me wrong, many of the guys I was incarcerated with just pissed their time away, bitching about this or that and waiting to be released. I was asked many times in prison, "Why are you doing all this?" My reply was always, "Trying to figure my shit out!" It seems to me if you can't thrive in prison, it's unlikely you will thrive in the free world.

A friend let me borrow her car, and I took the driver's test and got my license back. She had an old-school Cadillac Eldorado, and as soon as I parallel parked it, the instructor said we were done. My mom helped me out with some money to buy a used car, and after six months, I saved enough to get a one-bedroom apartment on Oakridge Drive in Orlando. At twenty-five, I had my first place on my own. Evenings in my apartment playing some music, just sitting in a chair in solitude, and sleeping with both eyes shut felt great. For the first time in my life, I could truly relax in my own space, with my own rules. It was a dumpy apartment and the cheapest furniture, but it was mine. And my 500 square feet were perfect.

Work continued to give me a sense of stability, and I worked as many hours as they would give me. It felt safe. Work has always given me a sense of purpose, and the structure felt good. If I was working, it seemed less likely I would get myself in trouble.

The fear of returning to prison worried me a lot. The accident proved that one split-second decision could change everything. Before that tragic night, I was on a good path and felt pretty good about my future. And then I erased it all in a moment.

What would be different about this time?

Besides work, I didn't do very much. I'd crashed so hard, and going to prison left me with no confidence in the free world. While I had learned to thrive in prison and dreamed about how amazing freedom would be, quite frankly, it was kind of disappointing, and I was pretty lonely.

"Freedom" is an interesting word. Physical freedom is the ability to move about without constraint. Mental, emotional, and spiritual freedom are personal constructs. True freedom is the result of my state of being. While incarcerated, I found myself completely free (at times), and in the free world, I often found myself imprisoned in my own self-erected beliefs. As my life expanded, my mental freedom was often compromised as I continued to create prisons in my mind. It would be decades before I truly understood and realized freedom in the deepest sense.

While I was enjoying some moments of peace, there were strong feelings of guilt, inadequacy, and just plain not belonging. That familiar feeling that something was missing was present in an even bigger way. Everyone in my world knew I was a convict that just got out of prison, and I regularly got asked about it and heard people talking about me. I often felt uncomfortable.

Maybe even more significantly, I was really afraid of my reactions. In prison, there were rules we lived by that were pretty clear. Plus, it was a relatively small population. In the free world, there are laws, but everyone seems to have their own rules, and I often felt like they were violating mine. It took time to understand and even longer to train myself not to react. It took a few years before I could be in a crowd and not be tense and looking for where the trouble would come from. It took a long time before I could let someone bump into me and not feel the need to push back.

I had never been very confident, but now the feeling of inadequacy was strong and constant. While many people found it "amusing" to know a convict, especially one who did time with

Ted, they always seemed to have some doubt about me. It was probably a combination of my doubts, their doubts, and me projecting my doubts on them.

Years later, I caught up with a friend from the hotel. She did the required background check to get on my visitor list and signed me out of work-release on my days off. She told me she felt kind of crazy to be hanging out with me and often wondered if there would be some headline about how I murdered her and buried her out in the swamps. That conversation confirmed that my paranoia wasn't just in my head. She admitted that she was still a little worried about being around me when we caught up years later.

After working in the hotel for about a year, I decided to go back to college. I wanted to build a better life, and a college degree seemed like the "ticket." It was also something I had left undone, and a part of me wanted to see if I could achieve a legitimate college degree. Overall, I was feeling unsatisfied with my life and the stigma of being a convict. It seemed logical that a college degree would help me fill the void within me. This would begin more than a twenty-year pursuit of achievement in hopes that it would silence that feeling that something was missing.

I went to the Valencia Community College in Orlando to take a placement test. A week later, I was sitting in the office of the placement counselor, and she informed me that I tested at a tenth-grade level in math and English. A feeling of surprise and disappointment came over me. I had a high school diploma from a well-respected Connecticut High School, scored decently on the SAT, and had notched a perfect score on the military ASVAB test. Plus, I had completed a two-year degree in prison. "Are you sure?" I asked. She reviewed the results with me and was sure.

What the hell? I asked myself.

She explained that I would need at least eight classes over a few semesters to be well-prepared as a freshman in engineering. Since I was all but broke, living check to check, and had to work full-time to survive, I signed up for night classes and began my journey.

I could have spent a bunch of energy in victim mode complaining about how the system failed me, and I couldn't even read, write, or do math at a high-school graduate level. I could have just given up on going back to college. The reality is that, although I had a high school diploma, I couldn't do high school-level work. It felt like a harsh lesson in the difference between appearance and reality.

Over the next few weeks, I battled with my doubts and fears. *What am I thinking?* often floated around in my self-talk. It was humbling to accept that I tested at a tenth-grade education. I needed competence in something that I could build on, not just a piece of paper I could hang on the wall. I committed to going back to school and promised myself that if I could accomplish night classes and work full-time, I would go back to college full-time.

Over the years, I've realized that our society loves to sell, and we seem to gobble up status symbols—titles, degrees, brands, the size of a house or bank account, all of it. I guess it makes ranking the mass of humanity easier. It also seems to promise we'll be able to sort out our own status. In reality, it seems more effective at creating endless amounts of lack, self-hatred, and self-doubt. The constant need to prove we belong to one group or another, rather than understand who we are and what life we desire, is a reliable source of insecurity. I was entirely unaware of it, but I jumped deep into this pool. I bought into the insanity that once I got my degree, 2.2 kids, owned a house, drove the "right" car, and vacationed in the "right" places, I would "arrive" and be okay.

So, there I was, working in the hotel fifty to sixty hours a week while taking two classes at a time in night school. I would allow myself to sleep a few hours a night, start my day in the kitchen at 4:00 a.m., do homework on my breaks, and leave work after lunch service around 3:00 p.m. I would go to class Monday through Thursday from 7:00–9:00 p.m. Caffeine was definitely my friend, but once in a while, I would fall asleep at my desk in class.

After a few semesters of straight As, I decided I was serious and set my goals to return to Connecticut and study Chemical Engineering at the University of Connecticut (UCONN). I had applied to UCONN in high school but wasn't accepted. So, it would be an accomplishment to get accepted and study one of the hardest curriculums. I thought attending UCONN meant that I could finally stop the running tape in my head that I didn't belong and was worthless. At least, that's the story I told myself.

At the hotel, I transferred from kitchen staff to banquet waiter because it paid much better. I got in with the department manager and took every shift she would give me, regularly working 90 or 100 hours a week. I also got into several other hotels and worked big events there. I needed to save as much money as I could to go to college for four years. For about eighteen months, I worked a lot and took my two classes every semester. I allowed myself three or four hours of sleep a night and pulled a lot of all-nighters. I was on a mission.

One night I came home from work and had a few hours before school. I threw some hamburger in a pan and sat down on the couch to study. It wasn't until the smoke in the apartment was thick enough to choke me that I awoke from my impromptu nap. My burger was beyond crispy, and my apartment—well, it never lost that smell. I was pushing myself—hard.

My life was entirely focused on my goal of earning a college degree. I decided this was necessary to reach my greater goal, so I did what I had to do. The truth is, if you want to know how far you can go, you'll have to risk going too far. Way too far. Sometimes, in pursuit of a good thing, we lean out so far that our current foundation feels like it might not support it. I was teetering on the edge. This wasn't the first time or the last I would teeter on the edge of collapse in the pursuit of something better.

At the time, I wasn't conscious of everything going on in my life, not that I am ever fully conscious of it all. I was in the middle of a relentless pursuit of the life I thought I needed to build. The truth is, I was running from my past at least as much as I was running toward a better future.

Taking care of my physical or mental health wasn't even on my radar. I had decided what needed to be done, and I did it at their expense. From time to time, I grabbed for some escape to help me feel better in the moment.

I was driving past the Chevrolet dealer one day and saw a brand-new 1989 white Camaro and stopped in. It didn't take long before I owned my first new car. The car I wrecked years earlier was a white Camaro. As I drove away in it, I couldn't ignore the feeling of happiness I had inside me. One more check on the list of accomplishments.

Along with that happiness, though, a small part of me thought, *What the hell are you doing? Another white Camaro in Orlando?* I seemed to have a fixation with going back and revisiting the points in my life where things went wrong to prove to myself that I could do it right this time. Maybe I thought that was what I needed to do to fill the void I felt.

As I neared the completion of my community college courses with straight A's, I applied to the Chemical Engineering program at UCONN and waited. I applied to a few other schools but didn't want to go anywhere else.

One day an official letter from the University of Connecticut was sitting in my mailbox. I was accepted on a conditional basis and had to go to the West Hartford regional campus for a year. If my grades were satisfactory, I would be allowed to move to the main campus in Storrs my sophomore year. Of course, I would have liked a full acceptance, but I was getting used to having to battle for everything. I had my chance, and I was going to do this.

TURN THE PAGE

"WELCOME TO GEORGIA," THE SIGN READ AS I CROSSED THE bridge on I-95 from Florida into Georgia. I remember letting out a big sigh of relief and feeling a little bit freer being out of Florida for the first time in years. While location doesn't change you, there was some sense of relief to leave Florida a free man.

It was the summer of 1991, and I was headed to Connecticut to begin classes. My stuff had grown a bit from the days of a laundry bag. I was driving a packed little U-Haul truck and towing my Camaro on a trailer. Having finished my community college classes, quit my jobs, and terminated my lease, I was turning the page to the next chapter.

Turning the page sounds so romantic, and there was certainly something cathartic about it. In reality, I was turning the page on the chapter of my life in which I caused a horrific tragedy, went to prison, and battled back to some semblance of normalcy. I am not sure how much of me was running from my past and status as a convict and how much of me was running toward something better. It was a tangled mess of both.

Hoping to lose the scarlet letter (or at least hide it well), I decided to go back to ground zero and start over again. "A redo," you might say. It's a curious habit I have of running back to my past and pushing through that discomfort. Thinking about it now, it seems pretty clear that my need to fill the void feels like unfinished business, and I head back to the "hole" to look for fill material.

My mom still had the house in South Windsor, so I moved in with her after arriving in Connecticut. During my time in Florida, my folks had divorced, and my dad was living in an apartment the next town over. It was just my mom and me. I quickly settled in and started classes.

I made the commute into West Hartford every day for classes. I was never late and never missed a class. My fear of failing again was a massive motivator. I knew how wrong life could go in an instant, and I used that to keep me focused.

I wasn't very outgoing and kept my head down and did my work. When asked about my story, I told people that I was out of the Navy and going back to school, which wasn't a lie but also not the whole truth. The Navy had discharged me while I was in prison with an Other-Than-Honorable discharge. They could have pursued charges as well, but I guess they figured the State of Florida had done enough.

My decision to keep my past a secret had several facets. Most significantly, I wanted to blend in and be seen, or not seen, just like everyone else. I didn't want to be identified by my past. I didn't want to be a convict. I'd seen the looks and awkwardness since release, and I wanted to lose the feeling of shame. Being a convict felt akin to being a third-class citizen, at best. While I seemed to blend in, shame remained my constant companion. It was like getting a new suit. Things looked better, but the same body tagged along.

My focus was intense, and I got straight As. Classes were enjoyable, and the confidence that I might earn a college degree began to grow. I didn't want to start over again, so I decided to do whatever it took. In the fall of 1992, I headed to Storrs.

I studied almost all the time. Once in a while, I would take a break to go hiking or skiing or go out with friends. Outdoor activities were good for me, and I enjoyed them. Drinking often turned into a bad situation.

There was a lot of stuff buried in me, and I often wanted to pick a fight when I had a few beers. I wasn't much fun to be around when this happened. Burying my past took energy, and it seems that a few beers would open up a floodgate to emotions I kept locked up while sober.

It took decades to unpack a lot of my internal stuff, and there's always something else to unpack. Thankfully I've done a lot of that work and am happy to report it's more than worth it. Uncovering your limiting beliefs, false stories, and disempowering habits is not simple or easy, nor is reformatting them into your truths and empowering habits. In my experience, it seems like the only way to truly have peace and harmony.

For the most part, I kept my head down and studied.

At Storrs, I got a research assistant job working twenty hours a week to help pay the bills. I took all the loans and grants available to help make ends meet. I continued to live with my mom because I didn't have enough money to live on campus. In my experience, if your why is strong enough, there is a way to get what you need.

Classes were tough, and most nights, I left campus late at night and would be back at 7:00 a.m. with an hour round-trip commute home. On weekends, I would study all day. I found peace in the work because it kept me from thinking about anything else and out of trouble. I guess I have always found peace in the flow of work for that reason.

Hiding my convict past took conscious effort. I had to keep my "story" straight, which frequently created internal friction and anxiety. Hiding my past was uncomfortable, but sharing it was worse. Since my childhood, I've always hated rejection and often found it easier to be alone than face the possibility of it. While I was never a very social person, this further fueled my solitude. Even in social situations, I felt isolated in a way that I never anticipated. The internal friction from living a fabricated story was constant but (I told myself) necessary. While I was doing some work to clear up some of the faulty framework in my being, I was also creating a whole new messy framework.

In my sophomore year, I had a teaching assistant who was really cute and easy to get along with. I found myself seeking help more often just so that I could see her. She was a PhD student in Chemical Engineering, was really smart, and loved the outdoors. It took quite a while for me to ask her out, as I was fearful that my past would get in the way of someone as smart and accomplished as her. My confidence was still really low, and I was worried that once she found out I was a convicted felon, she might not talk to me anymore. It didn't help that I hadn't dated much since I was a teenager.

That winter, I finally asked her if she wanted to go skiing with a friend and me. She said yes. It wasn't long before we were dating. We both studied a lot but found time to go on hikes and spend time together.

Early in our relationship, I told her about my criminal past, and to my relief, she seemed okay with it. It was uncomfortable for me to tell anyone about my past, but especially early in dating. The insecurity of early courtship only magnified the uncertainty of my past. I figured it was better to get the potential rejection settled sooner rather than later. Of course, her acceptance was a relief. We agreed that in the life I was building, it was better to keep my past to myself. And so, I put my past back in the basement and moved on.

The summer between my junior and senior years, I took the summer off to drive across the country and visit national parks on my own. Most nights I spent camping in National Forests for free and sitting next to a campfire alone. My mom and dad came out and spent a week with me, and toward the end, my girlfriend came out, so we could spend a few weeks hiking in Colorado. I loved being out on the road with nothing more than a basic idea of where I was headed.

I've always been drawn to the vastness and freedom of the outdoors in a primal way. From my early teens, I have hiked and backpacked. Being out in the wilderness has always been a beautiful experience for me. Long before studying meditation and learning to quiet my mind at will, I found tranquility in the wilderness. Hiking and enjoying a campfire allow me to completely relax and be at peace. A long walk on a quiet beach feels rejuvenating. The chatter in my mind subsides in the temple of the outdoors. The fresh air, peace, and freedom I feel in the wilderness are revitalizing. This trip was the reset I had long dreamed about in prison. Being someone who, to this day, charges hard, the recharge of the outdoors is still priceless.

In my senior year, I decided I would go to graduate school, and all my advisors urged me to attend another school because they thought it would be incestuous to stay at UCONN. I applied to a number of schools and got accepted to all of them for the PhD program. I selected Clemson because they had a well-paying master's degree program. Besides, I was already thirty and wasn't so excited at the potential of still being in school at thirty-five if I went the route of a traditional PhD program.

This, of course, left my girlfriend and me in a difficult position, but we were both pursuing careers and agreed to make it work. On a limited budget and pre-internet, this proved to be more difficult than we thought.

I graduated at the top of my class from UCONN. This was a big win for me because I finally finished something meaningful and difficult. I was the first in my family to go to college and graduate. I had come back to Connecticut and graduated from UCONN, a legitimate school. My résumé was real.

While graduating felt like a real accomplishment, it didn't fill the void, which was disappointing, to say the least. A part of me expected some profound sense of wholeness to engulf me once I held that diploma wearing my cap and gown. Isn't that the "promise"?

Although it wouldn't become clear to me till much later in my life, it wasn't what I accomplished but who I became in the process that mattered.

The greatest thing I learned from my studies in engineering is how to frame a problem, evaluate it objectively with real data, and come to the best conclusion available. For a creative-minded person, this has been an amazing gift that has served me incredibly well.

On one of my last days at the University of Connecticut, one of my Chemical Engineering professors gave us some advice that has always stuck with me. He said that no matter where you go and what you do in work, somebody will always make more than you for what you perceive to be less work or intelligence. If you follow the "rabbit" down that hole, you'll always be dissatisfied. I am not sure there is a truer statement.

Now, decades later, I'll elaborate on his message a bit. No matter where you are and where you end up, no matter how much you have or don't have, there is always someone who will seem to have more than you. Don't waste a single ounce of your energy on this. It will never bring you joy or fulfillment. Truth be told, there is also always someone who has overcome more, worked harder, and grown more. Don't waste your energy on this either. Focus on your journey, your contribution, and your evolution, and consistently be a better version of yourself. Dig deep, chart your own course, live your most extraordinary life, and let them live theirs. Do what you can, with what you have, where you are.

With a growing résumé, a great girlfriend, and my freedom, things were looking up. And still, the emptiness inside me was ever-present. In fact, it was disappointing that with such great things happening, I was still feeling a deep emptiness, the same emptiness that had been with me since I was a little boy. Only now, I had added shame and guilt as core feelings. I was doing a great job of achieving, but the emptiness inside persisted. Despite evidence to the contrary, I refocused my energy on the next accomplishment.

At this point in my life, it never really occurred to me that the void I felt was an internal issue that the outside world would never fix. I bought into the fallacy that accomplishment, others' respect, and stuff would resolve my internal problems. It occurred to me that I didn't deserve any real peace because of what I had done, so I never spent much time looking for it inside. I simply kept working toward the next big accomplishment. In the grand scheme of things, this isn't the worst habit to have, but it didn't address the core issue. Each accomplishment felt empty because I felt empty.

At Clemson, I worked hard and was very successful. I graduated in the middle of the class. The theoretical work began to push my intellectual ability, and I was burning out on school and studying. My drive was intense, and I rarely took a break, which I now realize wasn't the healthiest or most productive way to live. I was running from failure, terrified that if I let up, if I failed, then I would be a failure forever and fall back into something or someplace I didn't want to be. It was a great motivator, but one that often left me feeling out of sync.

I had some friends at Clemson, and we would walk downtown on most Friday afternoons and let off some steam, often closing the bars and wandering home. Saturday mornings, I would be right back at it. It was interesting that my anger and tendency to want to fight had dissipated a good bit. I was starting to build some confidence and internal peace. It seemed like I didn't need to lash out at the world to release the internal friction that had dominated me.

I graduated from Clemson in 1997 with a Master's Degree in Chemical Engineering and went straight to work. Just like all my other accomplishments, it was a bitter-sweet moment that didn't deliver me the "promised land." With each job application, I was reminded that my hard work and hours studying didn't change my past. On paper, I was a successful graduate with glowing recommendations from advisors. I was also a convicted felon. Exxon offered me two positions right after graduation. They flew me to Houston first-class and courted me hard. This was a dream job for a newly minted chemical engineer! With the offer in hand, all that was left to do was formally submit my job application. Front and center was that single question: "Have you ever been convicted of a felony?" With a little research, I found out that Exxon did background checks and did not hire felons. The message was clear: *We don't want your kind around here.*

I ended up working for a large southern textile and chemical company, the firm that had sponsored my research program. They didn't hire convicted felons either, but I found out they didn't do background checks, so I took a chance and went to work, my secret still kept from everyone around me.

In the fall of 1997, I got myself a one-bedroom apartment in Spartanburg, South Carolina. From time to time, the world would remind me that I was a felon, and I continued to build a house of cards pretending that I wasn't. This was a lot easier in 1997, as the internet and access to the world's information weren't commonplace yet. But the emotional toll was still a heavy burden to bear. Rather than face those feelings, I did what I knew best: I dug in and worked really hard. I was convinced that I could outwork my past, change myself completely, and leave that story behind. I wasn't evolving as much as I was creating an entirely different life and persona.

I began to travel and build a research program to support the business, mostly high-end athletic and outdoor brands. It was interesting work and aligned well with my personal interest. I was an abrasive Yankee in a southern company, but I compensated for the feathers I ruffled with hard work and contribution. On top of that, I had a great boss who ran interference for me a lot.

My girlfriend and I were still doing well. Home for the holidays, we went to NYC to see *The Phantom of the Opera*, and during a carriage ride in Central Park, I proposed. And yes, she accepted.

6

ANGEL

On Friday, April 3, 1998, I was taking a class in New Jersey for work, and I got a call from Dad's next-door neighbor in Port Charlotte, Florida. "Bob, your dad is in the hospital. He walked into the neighborhood this morning in his PJs, delirious. We called the ambulance. I think you need to get here." I packed up my bags, drove to the Philadelphia airport, and hopped on the first flight I could get to Florida.

After I landed, I went directly to the hospital to see my dad. We weren't that close, but I was all he had left. To be honest, I was pretty irritated with the inconvenience of it all.

It didn't take long for me to see something in him I had never seen. The masks he had lived behind were lowered. There was a genuineness and compassion in his face I'd never seen. Maybe confronting the reality of death allowed him to be authentically present. It was immensely sad to see but powerful at the same time. I softened quickly, and with genuine love, I greeted him and asked him how he was doing.

He apologized multiple times—for what, I wasn't exactly sure. I didn't ask what happened but just listened. It was already late, and visiting hours were ending soon. He told me where things were in the house, and we said goodnight. I promised I would be there in the morning when visiting hours started.

I met with his doctor before leaving. The doctor explained that the best he could figure was that my dad overdosed, called the ambulance, and was taken to the hospital across the street. Then, while waiting on a gurney in the emergency room hallway, he got up and walked out on Thursday morning. Friday morning, he arrived in an ambulance at this hospital, pretty drunk and full of drugs. Although he was in rough shape, the doctor thought he was recovering well, and things would be fine.

As I pieced things together, the story seemed to be that my dad had walked out of the emergency room, went to a bar, and drank well into the night. The bartender must have given him a tab, and then Dad walked out on that. The bartender ended up at the house the next morning, banging on the door, wanting his money. My dad ended up sleeping in a ditch on the side of the road where a stranger found him. After waking up, he walked the five miles to his neighborhood in his PJs and slippers. What made the story even stranger was that my dad had quit drinking years ago.

It was eerie walking into his house. There was a feeling I couldn't place, but it was strong. It wasn't long before the neighbor knocked and told me the story again. I updated him on the situation at the hospital and went back inside.

The house was immaculate, as usual. On the kitchen counter, there were a large number of prescription bottles and a note. My dad was left-handed and had very distinctive handwriting, and I knew it was his writing. The top of the note said, "Hemlock Society," and below were times, counts, and drug names. *What the heck is this?* I asked myself.

I compared the drug names to the bottles lined up on the counter, and they matched. Hemlock Society? I broke out my computer and found that The Hemlock Society was a group that supported self-administered euthanasia. With a little more research, I found detailed recipes to euthanize yourself. A recipe on the web page was the recipe on the handwritten note on the counter, exactly. Then it hit me; it wasn't an accidental overdose—it was a planned suicidal overdose on doctor-prescribed medication.

As the idea that he planned to kill himself began to sink in, the foundation of my very existence wobbled. *Why would you do that? So calculated, so thoughtful.* The bottles were all arranged. Even after taking all the pills, the list and the bottles lined up neat and tidy. This was my dad. He planned, organized, and executed his self-destruction. There is a strength, a foundation in the very sanctity of life, that those moments stripped from me. While logically, I was fully aware of suicide, this was my father. He brought me into this world and decided to leave it this way? How does one make sense of this? I knew he struggled. I knew he was often depressed. None of that filled the emptiness that was left when I realized he systematically executed his own demise.

His apologies started to make a whole lot more sense. He hadn't considered having to confront me with this.

The next morning, I was at the hospital when visiting hours began, and we talked most of the day. I decided that morning that I wouldn't confront him about the note and pills because he didn't need my inevitable judgment. He continued to apologize, and we talked about getting his stuff straightened out and maybe selling the house and moving him to South Carolina to be closer to me. From time to time, his eyes would literally roll into the back of his head out of sight. It was the craziest thing. I guess I knew in my soul that he wasn't going to make it, but we continued to talk like he would.

In some regards, it seemed like he didn't want to die anymore. Maybe the finality of death was more than he realized. Maybe he didn't want to have to tell me he still wanted to die. He wasn't ever much of a fighter, and this didn't elicit much of a fighting response in him either. As we talked, he kept apologizing to me for this and how he treated me growing up. He just kept saying he was sorry.

It was the first time I had seen him truly remorseful. It was the first time I had ever seen him seem genuinely sorry about anything. It was the first time he let me "see" him. Maybe it was the first time he saw himself.

As I left that Saturday night, so many things were going through my head. I mean, I saw with my own eyes what it's like to view your life journey and not be at peace with it. Not be at peace with yourself. I saw what it means to die unfulfilled and unhappy with the life you lived. That, even in suicide, he had to face me and know that I knew. That couldn't have been easy. In a life flush with lessons, this was coming at me like a flood. I was not yet ready to digest or learn many of them, yet they would be crucial later in life.

The next morning, it was clear things were fading fast. He was in and out, but mostly out. The doctor said they didn't know what was happening. Dad and I had a few conversations, but nothing very deep as he wasn't "there" very often. I just sat with him. In the afternoon, a nurse came in and told me I should have him transferred to Tampa because he would die here with the level of medical care he was receiving. I said I would see what I could do in the morning, as it was a Sunday afternoon.

On Monday morning, things continued to deteriorate. The doctor said they wanted to do exploratory surgery to see if they could find the problem. In my soul, I knew my dad was ready to go. I consented. Before they wheeled him into the OR, I held my father's hand and kissed him on the head. He said, "I am sorry," and I said, "I love you, Dad. It's okay." He opened his eyes and said, "I love you too," through the tubes hanging out of his mouth. His hand squeezed mine, and I realized that I would likely never feel that again. The little boy in me still longed for my dad, and while this wasn't exactly what I wished for, it was closer than we'd ever been. The nurse led me to a private room where I sat alone. After a short while, there was a knock at the door, and the surgeon came in. "He's gone. He didn't suffer but went into cardiac arrest before we began and died immediately."

There it was. In a matter of a few days, my dad and I had gone to a place deeper than either of us had ever dared. And now he was dead. The brief glimpse of something that felt like authentic father and son, done. I sat there unable to speak, and the tears that I hadn't cried in years rushed out. The doctor was uncomfortable, said he was sorry for my loss, and asked if I wanted to see my dad, and I nodded yes. He said he would be back once they cleaned him up and left quickly.

I just sat there crying as the puddle of tears began to pool on the table. The table that was holding me up. The grief was enormous, and I didn't fight it. I just let the tears flow as they needed to do. I couldn't remember the last time I cried. It's ironic that the death of the man who taught me not to cry had me crying gallons of tears. They were tears of loss, pain, and memories. They were long overdue. Maybe I cried for both of us.

I had stopped crying when the doctor came back. He asked if I was ready, and I got up and followed him. He explained there was still a hose down his throat, as there would be an autopsy to confirm the cause of death. We walked into a cold room and in the corner was a bed with a sheet over my dad's body. The doctor pulled down the sheet. My dad's face was chalky like dry stone and a greyish blue that looked like death. His eyes were closed, and the tube stuck out of his mouth, pointing into the air, no longer attached to anything. There was a stool next to the bed, and I walked over and sat next to his body. He wasn't there anymore, and I could feel the absence. The sound of silence made me wonder if the world had stopped. In a profoundly deep way, it had.

I took his hand and held it. The little boy desperately hoped that it would squeeze back, but it didn't. I have come to appreciate the grasp of the hand, the feeling of life, and the connection that a simple holding of hands can convey.

The body that lay on the table didn't have any squeeze remaining. I sat staring at his face—at death—for a long time. I knew I would never see him again, and it was really hard to get up. Finally, I looked at his face one last time, kissed him on the cheek, and said goodbye. I walked to the nurses' station and asked if I needed to do anything. They asked if I knew where I would like his body taken, and I didn't. I would have to figure that out. I walked out of the hospital alone. Without a father.

In the days that followed, I went through my dad's files in his office to see if I could piece together the state of his affairs. In a folder marked "death certificates," I found my grandfather's death certificate. I had never met my grandfather as he died before I was born. I only knew him from a single picture of him sitting in his chair displayed in my grandmother's living room when I was growing up. No one ever said much about him. I read through it. Death at fifty-four years old. Cause of death: suicide by salicylic acid and alcohol poisoning. An intense chill coursed through me. My dad was fifty-four. Suicide. Pills and alcohol.

This was all news to me. It turns out that my dad was fourteen years old when his dad killed himself in 1957 by swallowing an entire bottle of aspirin and washing it down with a slew of booze. There were so many questions. What did this all mean? Had my dad waited till fifty-four?

I'd lost my father to suicide and found out his father took his own life as well. Both fifty-four. I was thirty-three, so this didn't seem pressing at the moment, but it certainly felt like a dark fog settled in over me. At the very least, it was a revelation that perhaps I wasn't the only one in my family who felt like something was missing. In fact, it felt more like a family tradition to live a life haunted by an inner darkness. Whether or not I knew it at the time, this was my first sign that the cycle might continue if I didn't resolve the emptiness I felt. These were feelings I wasn't going to be able to outwork or outrun.

My dad mentioned a woman at the pharmacy where he went, and I went to talk with her one morning. She was very sweet and told me how my dad was always talking about me and how great it was that we emailed each other every day. I just nodded. Dad didn't have a computer or an email address, and we had never emailed. We rarely talked. In the end, he still lied to fill in the things that he thought were important. Another sign that I was repeating the patterns of my father...and his father before him.

One positive that came out of my conversation with the woman at the pharmacy was knowing the idea of a relationship with me, a connection with me, was important to my dad. I remember going out to my car and sitting in the parking lot for a while. Why had we been so distant? Why couldn't we connect? Why continually tell the pharmacist of our connection but not reach out to me?

When I was young, all I wanted was a connection with him, to feel accepted by him for who I was. But I never felt that. I guess he couldn't do that for me, in part, because he couldn't do that for himself. But I was too naïve to know that. As I got older, I got irritated and had no time for him or his drama anymore. I felt like I had been cheated and didn't give him the time or compassion necessary to understand that he had his own struggles and had been through his own hell, most of which I was completely unaware of. I felt like it was my father's responsibility to be the adult. The truth is, I was just as damaged and just as unable to go deep and connect as was he. To feel, share, and be authentic was nearly impossible for both of us. It wasn't until that Saturday, with death looming, that he could open up to me and let me see him. It wasn't pretty, but it was authentic.

Those last days were a true gift. I didn't fully appreciate it at the time, as it came so fast. But, as I've worked to bring down the barriers he and I shared, I've seen the beauty of those last moments. Not many fathers and sons are given that kind of opportunity, especially with the relationship we had.

It's so easy to judge people and think you know their story. But I never knew my father's story and couldn't possibly understand his journey. I just thought he was the parent, and he was supposed to know how to be there for me.

As I put his story together, it humbled me in many ways to see how little I knew about my own father and his struggles. In many ways, my father became human in those final days and the days after his death. No doubt that it got even clearer as the years went on, and I would finally have to face my own struggles.

Another big lesson from all this was that I saw with my own eyes that people are all doing their best with their experiences and what they are capable of today. I don't think anyone wakes up and says, "I am going to underperform my capability today." It's quite likely I have no idea what it's like to walk their journey, and any judgment I pass on them is nothing more than a projection of my own shadow.

By getting to see deeper into my father, I got to look in the mirror. I was my father's son in many ways. I wasn't ready to accept it at that point because it scared me, and I had no idea what to do with it. Could I change? Was I doomed to repeat? Could I actually be more authentic and connect with others? Although I wasn't ready to explore the answers at the time, it was important to ask the questions. Real change begins with a search, and the questions were the beginning.

I had my dad cremated. The burial service refrain, "Earth to earth, ashes to ashes, and dust to dust," didn't prepare me for the moment when they delivered my dad's ashes in a small box. I carried his ashes back to Spartanburg and then back to Connecticut and buried him next to his mom at the family plot on the hill.

My grandfather, grandmother, and father, all tortured souls in their own right, lay next to each other. I sat on the grassy hill overlooking the cemetery for a long time that afternoon, hoping that death had brought them all peace, but I knew that it had not. I decided that I would not be buried at this place; it didn't feel like a peaceful place. I wanted my ashes spread somewhere beautiful and peaceful, with no marker. Earth to earth, ashes to ashes, dust to dust. I want my legacy to tell of my journey, not an engraved stone. I realized that, more than anything, I wanted to truly rest in peace.

MEETING MY SON

Once I returned home from Dad's burial, I resumed my "normal" life. True to form, I threw myself back into work. Processing and fully coming to terms with what had just happened would take time—decades—but it was a blessing to get those last few days with my dad.

I was just beginning to unpack and grapple with his suicide and the broader concept and implications of generational suicide.

The chasm in my life seemed to widen overnight, and the void within me grew deeper. It wasn't something that I could just "handle." To be honest, I hid the generational suicide piece as well as I did my crash. Another string in the tangled web I was weaving.

Unfortunately, busy schedules, family trauma, and long-distance relationships don't mix well. It wasn't long before my fiancée and I broke up. We had drifted apart after a few years of a long-distance relationship.

After we broke up, she told me that I seemed more interested in the concept of marriage than in actually being married. I think what she meant was that I wasn't emotionally available, and while I denied it at the time, today, I can clearly see the depth in that truth. I wasn't emotionally available to myself or her in many ways. The truth is, I didn't trust people, especially myself, and it's impossible to have a deeply meaningful relationship with another person when you don't have one with yourself.

In a short period of time, I lost my dad and fiancée, and that hurt a lot. I remember feeling a real sense of abandonment and confusion. Being unavailable to myself or others didn't make it hurt any less. It was a difficult time in my life, and I spent a lot of time in the mountains, hiking and fly-fishing in solitude, trying to sort it out and searching for some peace.

As I began to date other people, a pattern began to emerge. People in pain, who are searching for something outside of themselves, tend to find each other, maybe because we assume our missing pieces will align and everything will be right. While sometimes these relationships can work, in those years, that wasn't the case for me. It seemed like endless drama and infidelity. Rather than examine my part in the dysfunction, I typically blamed my partner and ultimately gave up on the idea of passion. I figured a calm home life was the only way I would realize my ultimate search for peace, so I stopped looking for the fiery relationship that seemed to attract me.

At this point in my life, I wasn't intentionally subjecting myself to the many things causing friction in me and my life. I was unaware of most of them. The framework of my very existence had so many conflicts and fallacies that I was in constant turmoil, yet I still thought if I worked hard enough and achieved enough, it would all get better. Of course, that is akin to building a bigger house on a faulty foundation and hoping for the best. The constant inner turmoil drove me to need more escapes.

And then one night, while out seeing a live band in town, I met the woman who would become my wife. Our relationship didn't start with a bang, as my previous ones had, but we were great friends and didn't have much drama. Marrying her felt like the right step forward. With my personal life in "order," I was one step closer to the complete life I had been chasing for well over a decade at this point. We were married, and shortly before my fortieth birthday, my son, Collin, was born.

There are defining moments in life. The moment that Collin emerged into this world was one of them. It wasn't an easy birth, and he wasn't breathing, but it was magical. In very quick order, he was breathing, and with his first breath, let out a scream that told the world he had arrived.

Like many other parents, I decided I wasn't going to be anything like my father, and I would be the father I always wanted. Of course, inside, I was scared as hell. *What do I know about being a good father? How will I raise him?*

Maybe some parents are ready for their first child, but I was not. Like many things in my life, I loved the idea but had no clue what I was getting myself into and had no idea what I didn't know. I was afraid to break him and made the mistake of thinking logic would work with an infant, and well, it didn't! No matter how much I bartered with him, he carried on doing what he needed to do.

A child is always telling you something, and often, it's not what you think it is and more often not what you want it to be. Sounds pretty obvious, but it wasn't to me. To say I was stressed would be an understatement. Plus, I was completely exhausted. Collin didn't sleep through the night for his first five years, so sleep was not something I experienced in any abundance for a long stretch.

Early on, maybe a month or so, my wife and I decided to alternate nights taking care of him so that at least we slept every other day. One night, I was trying to console Collin, and the only way I could find was to rock him gently as I walked around. He would fall asleep, and after a while, I would sit down in the recliner in his nursery. Boom! He would wake up and cry. So, I was up and walking again. Around 3:00 a.m., I was exhausted when he started to cry again. I thought, *I totally get how people shake their kids too violently and hurt them. I am not going to do that, but I get it!* The cold chill that overcame me was terrifying. I held this precious being in my arms, and part of me just wanted my current nightmare to stop so that we could sleep. I think I walked around the house for the next four hours while he slept without issue as penance. It was a profound moment, though. How often have I judged people for doing things that were wrong and later ended up in a situation where all of a sudden, my narrow-minded self-righteousness was ripped open by my current reality.

Getting married and having a child didn't fix me or any of my ineffective conceptual frameworks. Actually, it just put more stress on them, me, and almost everyone around me. The suffering I was experiencing was a result of the massive confusion in my mind. At the core of my dysfunction was the incredibly disempowering belief that I was supposed to know what to do, and yet the situation I found myself in over and over again indicated I was all but clueless. It felt like I had no idea how to be a loving partner or parent, and jumping into both just created more and more internal friction. With my partner, it was easy to shift the blame. With my son, it wasn't. There is no doubt he taught me more about myself than I ever taught him.

As had always been the case, my body was a reflection of my being. My growing waistline signaled the stress I was feeling and my escape through food and alcohol. While I had gotten into great shape and even run a four-hour marathon since my breakup with my ex-fiancé, the old habitual grooves in my mind of eating and drinking to escape were now back in full force. It wasn't long before my body slipped from healthy and in shape to fat and out of shape once again.

In 2007, our little family moved to Park City, Utah, for a new career opportunity. We found an amazing log cabin up in the mountains and tried to build a life on the other side of the country. My job was going well, and our place in Utah was pretty close to my dream situation. Pretty close wasn't good enough, though. Although I fully embraced fatherhood, my relationship with my wife wasn't working for either of us. We tried counseling as a last-ditch effort to keep things together.

On top of couple's therapy, I tried a few sessions on my own. One session, I remember vividly. During the session, I was telling the counselor that I thought things would be different. I worked hard, went to college, got a great job, got married, had a son, and yet, I still felt this big void and felt like a failure. I thought I would have "arrived" by now, figured "it" out. She looked at me without much reaction and said, "Yeah, you and every other successful, middle-aged guy that walks into my office."

I paused for a minute and said, "What? Are you serious?" A part of me wanted to scream, and the other wanted the answer to the riddle. I didn't scream, and to my disappointment, she didn't have the "answer" to the riddle of life I found myself in either. At first, I found some comfort in knowing I wasn't alone. It didn't take long before it all just seemed to irritate me more. *Why is this such a secret?* I wondered.

In dark moments the voice inside my head would increase in volume and tell me I must be broken. That I was the only one who couldn't figure my life out. I was doing my best with the frameworks and tools I had at the time, but my life just wasn't working very well.

Counseling wasn't helping my marriage too much. We couldn't contain our frustrations, and the signs started to show up everywhere.

One morning, I sat at the kitchen counter with Collin, and he accidentally spilled some milk. His immediate reaction was sheer panic. He started to cry and apologize profusely, and I saw a level of fear in my child that broke my heart. *How did we get here? I mean, it's a glass of milk.* At that moment, I knew in my soul that I needed to get my act together and raise my son on my own. There are moments in life when the chasm of your true reality opens up, and you just know something, and this was one of them. By late 2008, my wife and I called it quits.

As part of the divorce settlement, I received sole custody of Collin and became a single father with a pretty pressing career. My mom was living in Salt Lake City and helped me through the transition. Although it wasn't an easy adjustment, as always, my mom helped out. And my top priority was being the kind of father Collin needed. I had done difficult things my whole life;

this was more important than any of those past accomplishments. I knew I would do what needed to be done to raise Collin in a healthy environment.

There were many moments when the delusion of how my life was supposed to turn out would hit me. Mid-forties and a single parent. I kept thinking about what I wanted life to look like, and this wasn't it. Early one morning, Collin woke me up and said, "Dad, I don't feel well." As I opened my mouth to ask what he was feeling, he projectile vomited directly into my mouth. *Message delivered!* Within twenty-four hours, we were both in bed with some kind of flu and a high temperature and wearing the bathroom out. I felt so inadequate as a parent in times like this, but I always kept moving forward and did the best I could. He deserved at least that.

8

PROMISED LAND

Against the backdrop of my father's death, a broken engagement, building a small family, and becoming a single father, my career continued to move forward. Driven by the same need to prove myself as I'd always felt, I continued to push hard in terms of professional accomplishments.

In 2001, I applied to Duke University for their Executive MBA program (at Fuqua) and was accepted. I thought maybe one more degree would sort things out. The campus was drivable from my home in Spartanburg, so I attended classes in Durham every other week for two years. I loved school, and my classmates were all really smart people. It felt great to be surrounded by a group of impressive teachers and students and realize that I fit in. I truly appreciated the intelligence, vision, and sheer potential I experienced there.

I've always been curious and, when I was interested, loved to learn. As I continued to surround myself with smarter and more driven people, I was inspired and motivated by their capacity and contribution. It was also humbling, in a very healthy way.

The convicted felon with a tenth-grade education attending community college at night when he was twenty-five years old was often amazed to have earned my seat at Fuqua. I was also very impressed with many of those around me. At Fuqua, I had the immense privilege to be around people who were thinking and executing at a level beyond my current ability to imagine. It was a profound time in my life when I'd earned my seat at the table of very smart people, realized I belonged, and was completely comfortable with the fact that I wasn't the smartest, most driven, or most capable.

One of the people I met at Duke made a lasting impression on me. He was in his thirties, a medical doctor, earned a Georgetown law degree, and was at Duke getting his MBA. He said he always wanted to help people, but his reach as a doctor was small. He decided to get his law degree plus an MBA to be a venture capitalist and mentor and fund startup medical companies to expand his reach and increase the number of people he could help. He was an amazingly down-to-earth person who seemed to be achieving his grand vision while still making time to play volleyball on the weekends. I have met a few people like this in my life who truly redefined what was possible for me. They inspired me to continue to expand my vision and execution across all the facets of my existence, to go deeper and continue to push myself on my journey. Their inspiration has contributed to the man I am today and the man I will become tomorrow. Their inspiration has contributed to me continuing to jump into the deep end of unknown waters and work really hard.

My job in South Carolina was going well. I was promoted to manage our newly developing military business. The president and CEO of the company at the time was very interested in this.

He was a legendary industrialist, businessman, and political activist; it was a real privilege to work for him. On multiple occasions, I got the chance to spend time with him and learn from him, many of the lessons that I have, over the years, come to appreciate more and more.

As part of my role, I was lobbying on Capitol Hill for military funding. Once a month, I would spend a few days in DC, visiting senators and congressmen and having dinners with admirals, generals, and some of Washington's power brokers. I had a favorite hotel and always scheduled the trip to coincide with our law firm's once-a-month intimate dinner for its key clients in DC. I remember sitting in Senator Lindsey Graham's office having an in-depth conversation with him about the science we were developing for the Army and NAFTA trade policy and, at the same time, thinking, *Is this really happening?*

Despite working tirelessly and securing millions in federal funding my first year, my career at Milliken came apart in a hurry. The military business was going well, and everyone seemed pleased. But then the drama started. The president, who I reported to, began having an obvious affair with a much younger associate. Unfortunately for me, the young associate and I had a brief relationship prior to this. The president was asking me to do wildly unethical things, and when I finally went to HR, the news traveled to the president, and my career burned out pretty quickly after that. Despite being offered the option to move to another division, I decided that the company and I were no longer a fit and moved on as it was obvious that I was no longer part of that "boys' club." I went from flying high to pulling the ejection seat in a split second. While the situation I found myself in was less than optimal, I now realize I contributed greatly to the whole messy affair. I ruffled a lot of feathers as the young, brash man that I was, which is much clearer looking back now than it was back then on my self-righteous little podium.

I quickly found a role working for a nonprofit defense contractor in Kentucky. As director of sales and marketing, I got a sweet incentive-based job, took my contacts, and got to work. This was an interesting time during the Iraq war. We were part of the government's AbilityOne program. Our mission was to employ, as 85 percent of our workforce, those with severe handicaps, for which we received preferential treatment on government contracts. It took me about six months before I brought in $30 million in new sales, an amount that almost doubled the company's size.

By 2007, the U.S. Government was starting to crack down on military supply chain abuse—a process they had turned a blind eye to for the previous five years. When we went to war in Iraq, the military supply chain was not prepared. Headlines read that our soldiers were going into combat without a helmet or body armor, and the government pushed the companies in the supply chain to do whatever it took to get things done. No taxpayer wanted to hear about supply chain rules preventing our soldiers, our kids, from getting the equipment they needed. By 2007, things shifted. Government agencies were coming around to scold everyone for doing things that weren't by the book—things they were encouraging five years earlier.

The situation fascinated me and reminded me of what I'd done more times than I cared to count. The military supply chain wasn't prepared for war because no one had been planning for a war. When the headlines started pointing fingers at the government for sending our soldiers to war without the appropriate gear, the government's immediate reaction was to abandon all the contracting rules! "Just get us what we need" became their new motto. Later, as things calmed down and the headlines went away, they quietly, and not so quietly, came around and scolded us. It seems like the authentic thing to do would be to say, "We weren't ready for this and are suspending the rules," and later reinstate the rules in some orderly fashion. I wish I could say that I never did this in my own life, but I'm sure most of the people who've been part of my journey would surely laugh at the irony if I did.

That's not to say that senior management of the nonprofit wasn't taking advantage of the situation, with little focus on getting it right. As I started to get a clearer picture of what was going on, I realized the extent of what we were doing, and it didn't align with who I was. I wanted to earn success, but I needed to do it the right way. In the very next board meeting, I decided to resign on the spot. Years later, the FBI interviewed me about my time with the company, and after reading that I resigned in protest, moved on to others in the organization.

I came home that night and told my wife that I had resigned. We had only been living in Kentucky for ten months and had barely finished unpacking. This was the beginning of the end for our marriage. The strain of our situation was more than our fragile relationship could handle at that point.

I started a consulting business out of my basement and quickly got a few job offers. That's when I decided to run a small company for some venture capitalists in Salt Lake City, Utah. That's how our little family ended up living in Park City.

When I accepted the job in Utah, my résumé began with UCONN, and no one asked me about my past. I started to feel comfortable that I had put enough space between my past and my new life. Then, in 2008, I was flying into Calgary, Canada, for a big meeting. As I went through immigration, I was pulled aside and escorted to a room. An immigration officer asked me if I had ever been in trouble. Surprised by the question, I said that I had. He informed me that Canada did not allow convicted felons to enter the country, and I was attempting to enter illegally. My passport was seized, and I was allowed to stay in the hotel in the airport until my return flight in the morning. They were deporting me. But not without hours of conversations and forms. Turns out that due to 9/11, they were now running the full manifest of all flights coming into Canada, and I had been flagged. Once released, I had to call my boss, tell him the full story, including the fact that I would not be able to attend the meetings or enter Canada again, at least until I tried to regain my right to enter through some lengthy, legal process.

That night, I sat in a hotel room by myself, and the truth of my past came rushing back at me. "An immense case of imposter syndrome" would be a good headline for what I was feeling. I had made a ton of progress since getting out of prison—not a single bit of trouble outside of a few minor traffic tickets, three college degrees, completely self-supported, a father—but that night, none of it mattered. I was a convict with a seized passport, sitting in a hotel room in a foreign country waiting to be deported. In many ways, my foundation felt so flimsy. I was an imposter living in a house of cards that always felt like it was on the verge of crumbling. My biggest fear—that I wasn't enough— came flooding back in that hotel room. I wasn't enough, and this proved that the little voice inside my head had been right the whole time. My void seemed to exponentially expand overnight!

It wasn't long after that incident that my time at that company came to an end. It was 2008, and the economy started to tank. By the summer of 2009, the company lost 50 percent of its sales. I did my best to stop the bleeding, but 50 percent of our sales came from steel mills, and they all shut down in a matter of thirty days. We all took pay cuts, but things continued to get tougher. Truth be told, I never got over the embarrassment of being deported, especially while working with a company owned by devout Mormons. Not only was I not a Mormon, but I was a convict who hadn't told the whole story of where I came from. I don't know if it was all in my head or not, but it dominated my thoughts.

In the early summer of 2009, I took a hard look at buying the company I was working for but knew, in my soul, the deal wasn't a good one for me, especially with the economic uncertainty we were in. At this point, my relationship with the VC group was challenged, and I was struggling to handle the travel schedule and be a good father to Collin.

One night, sitting in my kitchen, I decided to start my own company. It seemed like the only way that my past wouldn't be an issue. I thought I could be free from the fear of someone finding out and the shame that would follow because I would be the owner. Collin was getting older, and as a single parent, I needed more control over my schedule, over my own destiny.

On my laptop one night, I developed a name for the company and constructed the word SAPREX, SAP for sapience or wisdom, R for research, and EX for execution. I decided to move to Charlotte, North Carolina, to start the company. Charlotte seemed like a perfect location, as it was near the suppliers I imagined I would work with, which would keep the supply side of my travel to a minimum. I flew to Charlotte and bought a house outside of the city in Gastonia in a weekend. In early August, Collin and I moved to Charlotte.

In a matter of six months, I got divorced, became a single parent, quit my job, moved across the country, and started a company.

My "company" was no more than an idea when we arrived in North Carolina. The house I bought had a full basement, and I started there. I didn't have any lab equipment, customers, or at that point, even a legal company. So, I did what I knew how to do best—I jumped in with both feet, and I got to work and created one. I rented a truck and went on a road trip to buy some used lab equipment and built a small lab, complete with fume hoods in my basement. SAPREX would be a material research company, and I decided on a tagline: "Better Science Materialized."

As a single dad, my parenting goal was to make Collin's life as normal as possible. I made breakfast every morning, and he attended pre-school. I would pick him up in the afternoon, and we would spend time together until his bedtime when I would go back to work.

Initially, I had a few projects that I worked on developing and got a few paying research contracts, but all in all, it was really slow, and money was bleeding. I had self-funded the company and set a limit on how much money I would invest before I closed shop, just like my mentors taught me.

By late 2010, it started to look like SAPREX wasn't going to make it. I was down to my last $5,000, and my projects had all run into technical roadblocks or dead-ends. I began working on my résumé and decided to start looking for a job after the new year.

Just before Christmas, I got a call out of the blue from someone who wanted to talk to me about doing some research for his
company. At first, I thought it was a joke, but it became clear that
he was serious. I jumped at the opportunity and was soon working
late nights and weekends to develop a product for them, résumé
off the table.

In retrospect, there are so many moments in my life where
someone emerged or something happened that is so perfectly
timed and beautiful, I can't explain it as anything other than
divine intervention or a flow of life force that presented itself,
like someone throwing me a buoy when I was drowning. I mean,
I was about to close shop, and I got this call out of the blue from
a random engineer who had found my website, which was so
basic that *I* wouldn't have bothered to call me. This person said
in our first conversation, "I think you are exactly what we need."
Really? Is this a prank call?

I've been asked more than once, "Did you appreciate that in the
moment?" when I tell someone about one of my divine interventions. Well, rarely. For me, the dots are much easier to connect
looking back, and it's taken years for me to appreciate that. When
I am in the midst of chaos, I surrender to the things that life presents. Some of them turn out to be blessings, and others seem more
like brush fires. As someone blazing my own trail, I'm often out on
a limb of uncertainty, and I seem to be most comfortable there.
The key is I surrender to my journey and fully embrace all that
comes along. To say it another way, I kiss all the frogs and prin-
cesses that come along passionately. Most often, it's not till later
that I can tell which is which. It definitely makes life interesting.

"I get to do this!" is something that has also served me well. In
the depth of chaotic moments, especially when the storm seems

to be winning, or in the midst of a task I've done a thousand times, I remind myself that "I get to do this!" as opposed to "I *have* to do this." This form of appreciation is one of the tools I use to combat my tendency to see the potential downside of things or wallow in the "driving rain." If I am still upright and moving, there is something to appreciate!

The project quickly got the business cash-flow positive and staved off closing up. I jumped in and began to run trials and work with all the passion granted to me and made great progress. Needing more space and a legitimate facility, I expanded the operation from my basement to a lab on the campus of the University of North Carolina Charlotte and added a few employees. Things went well over the next two years as our product was approved by a major truck manufacturer, and SAPREX and our customer prepared for a big launch. And then our communication with the customer went dead. And the deadline passed. And the money stopped.

After some months, I learned our customer didn't get the business with the company they had planned on, and it would be another model cycle before we'd get another chance. Three years. We had a contract that allowed SAPREX to open the product to other firms, but our customer wanted no part of that. For me, SAPREX was back in survival mode, and our customer's lack of communication had me feeling very frustrated and worried. I felt like I had delivered my part of the deal, and they hadn't. I didn't understand why we had to play all these deceitful games.

Being an early-stage entrepreneur was incredibly stressful for me. I'd put all my eggs in this golden basket, and the bottom seemed to fall out as my work was tied up in contracts and joint ventures. Like everything in life, there are always two sides to the story. Survival, paying my bills, and providing for my son dominated mine. For them—well, I'm not sure.

At this point in my life journey, I was so focused on achieving some level of success and terrified of failure and what that would say about me. I wasn't immediately able to realize my ability to survive and how far I had come. Instead, I was back to feeling like my house of cards was again going to collapse. It felt overwhelming and, at times, almost too much. Of course, it wasn't, and life went on. What's clearer now is that as the stakes got bigger, the level of drama I created in my head did too. My reaction to a bad grade on a quiz in elementary school had not fundamentally changed, but its energy had massively increased.

What did I do? I decided to go into my backyard and dig. I rented some heavy equipment, moved a few mountains of dirt, and claimed a backyard from the forest behind my house. I needed something that felt like progress. I had started this company to control my future, to rid myself of the cycle of secrets and deceit, and here it was again. The progress I thought I had made seemed to vanish in the fog. I needed time to work through the inner turmoil. Building something with my own hands has always been my go-to when life feels overwhelming. Bigger problem, bigger project.

After this reset, I went back to work further developing the technology, dissolved our partnership between SAPREX and our customer, and went looking for a new customer for a much-improved version of the product we have previously developed. In late 2016, my new partner was awarded a big contract, and I had about thirty days to build a resin manufacturing plant and begin shipping product in January 2017. After years of working at it, I was finally going to deliver on all the work.

For months there was little time for anything but work. We were working 100-hour weeks, and I was sleeping on the floor of a lab we no longer used for a few hours most nights because driving home just didn't make sense. I would go home a few nights a week, but other than that, I worked around the clock and slept just enough to "function."

Food had to be delivered, and for the most part, I was hooked on energy drinks and coffee. It was less than healthy, to say the least, but I wasn't going to drop the ball on launching our new product with another major truck manufacturer. In retrospect, there were things I could have done better, especially for my own health, but there are opportunities that you either deliver on or you don't. There was no way that this one was going to pass me by without me giving every ounce of my body and soul.

Late one night, I was running a forklift in our new resin plant and cracked my head open on the forklift cage. I grabbed a handful of paper towels to keep the blood out of my eyes and kept going and never thought twice about it. There were a few looks from associates, but anyone that knows me wasn't surprised.

When someone suggests how "lucky" I am or how I had this or that advantage, I usually think about the number of 100-plus-hour weeks I worked, how many nights I slept on the floor or in a chair in my office, or how many times I considered if an injury needed stitches and how much blood I might lose if I didn't get them. I have achieved a lot, but there aren't many people who will stay in the fire for as long as I will. I truly believe that extremely hard work and sacrifice are the price for entry into the arena. If you need it to be easy or fair, don't expect much in return. You have no idea how far you can go until you risk going too far. Rarely is it actually too far.

My girlfriend was growing impatient with me and my lack of attention to her and our relationship. In reality, my focus was on making my company work and raising my son. She needed more than I could give at the time, and our relationship became intensely tumultuous.

By the spring of 2017, I had the plant running well, having never missed or even been a day late on a delivery. My mom had moved into our house and was taking care of Collin for the most part, and he seemed to be doing well.

Everything I had worked so hard for seemed to be coming together. Maybe I was finally going to arrive at the "promised land."

9

DARK DEAD-END

By April of 2017, we had been awarded a significant contract with the truck manufacturer, scaled up a chemical production facility, and were shipping product, but I was teetering on the edge.

I'd gained fifty pounds over the past few years and was running on fumes and completely burned out. My blood pressure was soaring, despite being medicated, and I occasionally had these blinding tension headaches; occasionally, I could not get off the couch. My body was telling me it had enough of my abuse and was screaming for attention. My son was missing me. My family was walking on eggshells because my temper would flare up over the smallest things or seemingly nothing. My long-time relationship was all but over. My house was a literal mess. I was suffering physically, mentally, and emotionally, and it felt like there was no way out. This was the life I created, for better or worse.

One Saturday afternoon, I was driving across town when a truck unexpectedly swerved in front of me. I slammed on my brakes and swerved off the shoulder to avoid a collision. Furious, I immediately began to chase the driver down. A few traffic lights later, I pulled up next to him at a busy intersection, rolled down my window, and verbally unleashed on the driver. I told him to pull over, so we could settle this. From under his seat, the young man pulled out his 45-caliber handgun, rested it on his lap, pointed it right at me, and flipped off the safety. I didn't stop or flinch. Never looking away, I pulled out my phone and called 911 on speaker, and when the operator answered, I described the situation, blatantly challenging the driver. The driver clearly saw I was "crazy," put his gun under his seat, and sped off despite the red light. To say I was wound too tight, would, of course, be an understatement. Yet, at the moment, I couldn't see that.

The chaos in my head just continued to escalate. I became my own worst enemy, berating myself and anyone else who came into my path of destruction. All too often, I exploded, unable to handle any more stress to my inner turmoil and seeking some outlet. The voices in my head that told me I was out of control just kept getting louder. The stakes seemed to just get bigger. On top of all of it, I was working even more, sleeping less, eating about as poorly as possible, and starting to drink more often. There was so much tension inside me that I unconsciously looked for people and situations that I could offload some of it on. I regularly blamed others for just about everything dysfunctional with me and my situation.

At work, I hired a company to install an epoxy floor in the offices of the plant I purchased, and a week later, we were starting to move furniture in when I noticed the floor was blistering. In a few minutes, I realized the whole floor was delaminating. I took a corner and peeled up about a four-foot section in a single piece. After getting the contractor back several times to attempt to remedy the situation and a few heated screaming matches that brought us no closer, I tore it all out and began grinding and polishing the concrete myself. After this long journey of company building, I was angry, frustrated, and embarrassed. I couldn't even move into SAPREX's new offices and decided to put this final task on my back and carry it over the threshold. I ground and polished concrete eighteen hours a day for about two weeks like a possessed mad man.

My intimate relationship of five years finally came to its endpoint, at least the façade of it. I knew what was going on for months but didn't want to admit it to myself. We met one night to talk about our situation, but "we" weren't there anymore. I threw in the towel and broke up with her. The reality is that I hadn't been much of a partner for quite a while, maybe ever, and she needed more than I had to give at the time. I guess it wasn't unexpected, but it hurt deeply.

The reflection in the mirror at fifty-one was not something I was proud of. The chaos in my head reached a constant roar. Personally, I was in the midst of a Category 5 hurricane. The pain was real, it was deep, and I needed relief from it.

I went back to my eighteen-hour days of grinding and polishing the floor because it's what had to be done.

In the early morning hours of Wednesday, May 10, 2017, I finished. After inspecting the floors and giving myself the sign-off, I wandered into what would be my office and poured a glass of bourbon that I never drank. There wasn't anything in the office, so I sat down on the floor.

I was being called there, but I didn't know why. The light from the full moon penetrated the windows, and the freshly polished black concrete had a deep and mysterious glimmer. The steel grey walls stood bare and solemn. It was a shrine to all my work and maybe my life, beautiful but empty inside.

The adrenaline that had fueled me for months was gone, and my physical body was done. "Total exhaustion" begins to describe what I felt, but just the surface. This was a total depletion that I could feel in my bones. It was as if all the energy and momentum that got me to this moment in life just ran out. I came to a stop.

As I sat there, I drifted into a darkness. It wasn't a worldly place or some dream—it was this place I'd never experienced. It was intense in its harsh simplicity, dark as a frigid, moonless night. Perfectly silent. It was as if I could see and feel everything, yet the universe stopped. It wasn't evil, just brutally empty. Perfectly simple.

It was a dark, dead-end—or "a dark night of the soul," as some would say. The road I was traveling on clearly didn't continue. The universe came together at that moment to let me know that the way I got here wasn't going to take me any further. The era of my life that got me to this point was over.

Things had to change, and the universe wasn't going to wait for me to figure it out myself. This moment was it. It was time for me to surrender to the truth that I wasn't working. I had pushed my fallacy as far as possible. It felt like the very foundation of my being was being touched, and the curtain on the façade of the life I had known ripped away. I sat there on that cold dark floor at the crossroad of existence. Going back to my previous being was not an option. Giving up wasn't either.

Up to that point in my life, I didn't consider myself spiritual; I rejected organized religion and chose to worship at the altar of achievement, public opinion, and form. I didn't acknowledge that I might have, or be, a soul, and anything beyond rational thought wasn't worth a second of my time. "That's all crap," I might have said.

So, here I sat on the floor, having entered another realm. My body came to rest, and the universe waited. It didn't wait long. I had no fight left. My ego had no fight left. I surrendered all that I had known and granted myself permission to let it all go.

In that moment, I fully accepted that the conceptual framework that defined me and my life thus far was tragically flawed and unworkable. Up to this point, all the ideas and beliefs I'd been exposed to (and mostly adopted unknowingly and without proof) had defined my life. One shaky or false belief piled on top of another. The lessons from my house of origin, stuff I picked up in daily life, in the penitentiary, and others I collected along the way defined me in some randomly "organized" way. It was a shaky framework at best. If it had been a real physical house, it would have had that bright yellow tape around it that said it was condemned and awaiting demolition. *DO NOT ENTER!* In that space, the façade that I defended with my life disintegrated, leaving the opportunity of a lifetime.

The universe invited me to immerse myself into the deep unknown that separated my current state of despair and my innate potential. On the other side of this unknown space was a conscious being aligned with my soul. On the floor sat a being with no more expectations or meaningless goals. It was as if the universe was inviting me to truly begin the journey of realizing my true self and my real potential. A potential that I had always felt but not yet realized.

I know this may sound a bit mystical, maybe even "crazy." There was an intense serenity in the experience that was beyond surreal. A lifetime of pursuing a "good" life came to a brutal stop and a truly amazing place of profound clarity. Up to this point in my life, I could have been in the running for the least spiritual and most practical person on the planet. On that night, it was as if the gates to transcendence opened. In a very short period, I truly accepted that I wasn't working and walked through the open gate to begin the journey of awakening my soul and living it. It was truly that magical. That profound.

After a few hours, the sun began to rise, and the darkness broke. I got up and felt amazingly grounded and infinitely lighter. My body was beyond exhausted, but my purpose going forward was crystal clear. I drove home, took a shower, and slept for a few hours. It was a deep sleep of resolve.

DON'T KNOW
WHAT I DON'T KNOW

"The only way that we can live is if we grow. The only way we can grow is if we change. The only way we can change is if we learn. The only way we can learn is if we are exposed. And the only way that we are exposed is if we throw ourselves into the open."

—C. Joybell

Moments of deep despair are amazing invitations to enter life's biggest chasms. Life's ultimate chasm. For a moment in time, the flimsy, egocentric idea of our identity collapses, and the opportunity to break out of the self-erected prison that torments our very soul presents itself. To realize the amazing potential that opens, we must passionately seize the opportunity. We must be ready to listen, learn, cleanse, change, rebuild, and connect with our soul in the deepest ways. The risk of ignoring the opportunity is too great, as it assures a future shackled to the very darkness that delivered us to the depths of despair in the first place.

In those early morning hours in perfect darkness, I surrendered, and my existence completely changed. I don't say this in some trivial way, like the many times before that I had resolved to lose weight, to be more attentive, to find my purpose, or "turn over a new leaf." It wasn't some "ah-ha" moment. There was no "light" at the end of the tunnel or feeling of joy. No miracle healing. The curtain that protected me from my self-identity was ripped open. I accepted that nothing within me or out of me was off-limits. It was like buying an old house in disrepair. I had no idea what lay ahead but fully embraced that I would do whatever it took to get the structure and workings of it all operating well and create the home I knew was possible, even if that meant burning it all down and building a new framework piece by piece.

Breakthroughs often begin with breakdowns. I had the breakdown nailed, so now it was time to dive into the chasm of my life. I'd have to jump into the search to enlighten my ignorance as to what I didn't know I didn't know, learn what I needed, realize my truth, and begin the process of transformation. I fully committed myself to the quest of true transcendence, although I wasn't conscious, just yet, of what that meant.

There was no plan or some great vision, just a deep knowing that I was committed to my quest of fully entering the chasm that lay before me. Nothing, and I mean *nothing*, was off limits. If something presented itself, I'd do it. If something called me, I'd go. If I needed to let go of something, then I'd cut it loose. I told myself, if I needed to burn the house to the ground, dig out the foundation, and start all over, then that's what I'd do.

When I woke up after a few hours of sleep, my body still carried way too much fat, my energy was non-existent, and my blood pressure was still soaring. The mirror reflected an abused body.

That reflection was the result of the journey that got me there, the dysfunctional life I'd been living. While my reflection wasn't something I was proud of, there was a new sparkle in my eyes that said, from this day forward, things will be different! I realized that I had a lot to lose, learn, and work to do. I also committed that one day the reflection in the mirror would reflect a me that was whole.

My first inclination was to get my girlfriend back and try a "redo." Fortunately, she slammed the door shut and moved on with perfect resolve. It was exactly what I needed, even though it would be quite some time before I completely accepted that.

If you resonate with the feeling that something is missing, feeling lost, or darkness itself, I understand. You are not alone. In my experience, my dark, dead-end created an opening to begin my quest for my truth. When I walked through the open gate, I had no idea what I didn't know or where I might find answers. I knew that others had found some level of enlightenment, so I figured if they had realized it, so could I. The key is to take the first step, remain open, embrace everything that appears as an opportunity to enlighten your ignorance and keep putting one foot in front of the other. You don't know what you don't know...until you do.

"The journey of a thousand miles begins with a single step."

—Lao Tzo

I had journaled before, typically in the tough times, and I started the routine again. I spent hours trying to fully understand what was happening and where I might go from here. It provided a necessary outlet. The slow rhythm of writing helped reel in my monkey-mind thinking a bit.

My first thoughts were that my relationships were my problem. Looking back, all my significant intimate relationships had lasted at least a few years and had all ended in the same wreck. My lack of availability led my partner to seek it somewhere else, and when things officially ended, I was crushed. Of course, this was a symptom, not the root issue.

Committed to the process, I first called the therapist who had counseled my ex-girlfriend and me for a while. He said that he didn't feel ethically comfortable seeing me after our breakup, but he suggested a few people that I could go see.

One morning, I found myself sitting in Randy's office, feeling nervous and excited. Randy is a psychologist who specializes in men's mental health. He began his career in family practice but soon realized that family issues often came down to the man's lack of emotional availability to himself and his family. We did the customary introductions, with me giving a fairly quick but in-depth overview of my life, issues, and current situation and him asking a few more probing questions.

"How will you know when we are done working together?" he asked with about ten minutes or so remaining in our session.

I sat and pondered for a bit, and in total sincerity, I said, "I am pretty broken; I am not sure we are ever going to be done."

"Let me give it a try," he replied. "When you are able to feel, put words to those feelings, and are able to discuss them openly, we will be done."

I let that sink in, and I knew I was in the right place. We started meeting weekly the following week.

As I was leaving, he handed me a book and asked me to read it. With a copy of *Finding Our Fathers: How a Man's life Is Shaped by His Relationship with His Father* by Samuel Osherson, I took my first step toward real progress.

Randy and his partner also ran men's groups focused on giving men a place to share and work with each other. He said it might be a while before a spot opened, but it could be a valuable place for me throughout my newfound journey. Luckily, shortly after meeting Randy, a spot did open up, and I joined a weekly men's group facilitated by Randy and Joe.

The combination of working with Randy and a weekly group where I got to see that I wasn't alone was powerful and exactly what I needed. I read everything he suggested, engaged openly in group, and continued to fully engage in our one-on-one sessions.

After reading Osherson's book and evaluating my situation, I thought I had shut down my feelings, didn't feel anything, and needed to begin to feel. Growing up in the 1960s and '70s, men weren't supposed to express feelings, and I was no different.

I began a feeling practice in my journal. At least once each day, I would write at the top of the page, "What do I feel?" For quite a while, my immediate response was, "I don't feel anything!" But I committed to writing a full page each day, and before long, I would fill up a page with what I was feeling. When I finished, I would read it and would often be surprised at what came out of me. It wasn't always coherent. It was real. But where was this coming from? I was convinced that I didn't feel anything, yet I had pages of emotional truths.

Another pivotal revelation during my emotional journaling was that I didn't even know many emotional words or what they meant. More broadly, I realized that I didn't know the meaning of many words and, more often than I wanted to admit, was incapable of truly communicating what I was trying to say. As Randy had said at our first meeting, "realize your emotions and put words to them." This started my practice of looking up and writing down words and their definitions, something that continues today. Rarely does a day go by that I don't look up the definition of at least one word and write out the definition that truly represents what I am trying to say. Now, you will often find me asking, "What do you mean when you use the word...?" to myself and others.

My physical health also needed a massive upgrade. At an early age, food became my first escape. I learned that if I ate enough, I relaxed a bit. Growing up, we were a family that ate better during the week, and the weekend was more of an indulgence. Unwinding on the weekend meant big meals and desserts. The big weekend meals were more loosen your belt, lay on the couch, and bask in the feeling of peace as your body worked hard trying to digest the feast. We were also a house where my mom was the steady breadwinner and cooked all the meals. The advent of easy, processed food resulted in a lot of Hamburger Helper and the latest modern processed "food" innovations for dinner during the week.

I remember the day when my dad came home with our first microwave oven. "This thing is amazing! You put the hot dog in, and in just one minute, it's cooked." Dad got it set up, and we all gathered around for the magic demonstration. He put a hot dog on a plate and placed it in the microwave. We watched intently through the window on the door like Apollo was about to land on the surface of the moon. Dad pressed the start button, and we watched. Nothing much happened...thirty seconds... forty-five seconds, and then BOOM!!! The innocent tube of processed meat exploded like a stick of dynamite contained only by the microwave walls. "Great invention, Dad," I said as we all laughed. Of course, this brought on leftovers and Hungry Man frozen dinners with the warm "chocolate pudding." Eating often centered on how quickly we could put something on the table rather than a way to fuel our bodies with nutrients, but like many things, we didn't know better at the time. Clearly, my relationship with food wasn't the healthiest.

Over the years, my health and weight resembled the winding curves of a mountain road: up and down, left and right. I tried many of the latest diets and exercise programs. Most of them worked for a while, and then they didn't. The truth is, more often than not, I used food as an escape and ate to fill the void, although I wasn't conscious of it. Discipline worked for a while, and then I would fall off the wagon, never quite sure where the wagon was headed anyway. I drank, sometimes to excess, and my body's reaction to even a little alcohol was to crave sugar, which I would often indulge in. Overall, my body was like my general state in life: I couldn't seem to find what I was looking for and once again was open to just about anything.

My health needed to get better, so I cut the junk out of my diet, began exercising, and slept a bit more. Since I was in pretty bad shape, it didn't take too much effort to make progress. The reality is that I had been in and out of shape many times in my life. I'd run a four-hour marathon and a bunch of two-hour half marathons, but had yet to find the key to any consistency. I began seeing references to fasting to Dr. Fung's book, *The Obesity Code*. I read the book, and it made total sense. I found my next step.

My initial response to fasting was the same resistance most people have when I discuss fasting: "I can't do that." But I committed myself to do whatever it took. I jumped into fasting, and before long, I was water-only fasting for thirty-six hours three times a week. I would eat dinner Sunday night and not eat again until Tuesday. I would fast all day Wednesday, eat Thursday, and fast again on Friday. This became my standard routine for more than a year. I felt great fasting with lots of energy, and my weight continued to drop. In February 2017, I weighed 284 lb. after an especially indulgent weekend, and in November 2017, I was maintaining 220 lb. and feeling much better.

With a long legacy of emotional eating, fasting appealed to me. It helped me evolve my relationship with food. After enough thirty-six-hour periods with only water, I was much better able to be conscious when eating. *Why am I eating this?* and *How is this serving me?* are a few common questions I asked myself. I now understand that it also aided my body in regaining some of its intrinsic function, in terms of hormones and biological processes, that I compromised by my long-term abuse.

I also began to fast for longer periods of three and five days for the deeper health benefits of autophagy, not the weight reduction but to give my body a digestive rest. After a few stints of longer fasting, my weight settled in at 205 lb. and has remained there since.

Today, I continue to fast in different formats each week. At least three times a week, I skip breakfast and only eat within an eight-hour period, fasting for sixteen hours. Once a week, I fast for at least twenty-four hours. Once a quarter, I fast for at least five days.

Things were getting better with counseling, my men's group, exercise, and diet, but I had been here before: let things slide too far, make some changes, and then once things get better, stop paying attention again. Back in 2011 or 2012 after a big breakup, I got in crazy good shape, hired a life coach, and made some great progress, only to find myself five years later, again, buying "big boy" pants, seemingly lost and once again disappointed in myself. I was missing something in terms of true long-term transformation. This time had to be different. I'd come to the point where I wasn't sure how many more deep crashes I could handle.

MY DATE
WITH DESTINY

I FIRST SAW TONY ROBBINS ON TELEVISION IN THE EARLY 2000s while flipping through channels one night. It was an infomercial featuring a big guy telling me that a better life was available to me. Sitting on the couch on a Friday night, feeling sorry for myself, with an empty pizza box on the floor and a few empty beer bottles on the cocktail table, this seemed like destiny. I remember thinking, *Am I really going to pay $49.95 for a DVD set to find a better life?* Ironic considering there was $20 worth of beer and pizza already in my gut. I ordered it.

I listened to the CDs many times over the years. The messages made total sense, yet while I felt better after listening, I didn't change much, if at all. But now it was 2017, and I was in a completely different mindset. I had experienced total darkness and was fully committed to enlightening my ignorance and realizing a better way of living and being. Figuring that this time might be different, I pulled them out and listened to the seven-day program again.

Fate has a funny way of showing up when you truly need it; Tony came to Charlotte in the summer of 2017, and I attended the one-day event. Tony came on stage around 4:00 p.m. and he went non-stop till about 9:30 p.m. "Let's just go for it," I remember him saying. His message resonated with me, and I was inspired after the event.

Not long after, I got a call from one of his salespeople and signed up for Unleash the Power Within (UPW) in West Palm Beach in November 2017.

I flew to Ft. Myers in early November on my way to UPW. I walked up to the AVIS counter to rent a car for the week. The gentleman at the counter joked with me about being Robert Goulet, and I commented that I never got much for having the name. I suggested that he should rent me the convertible Jaguar sitting there in the display space. To my surprise, he said, "Why not?" and for an extra fifty dollars for the week, I drove off in this gorgeous convertible Jaguar. Something just felt different.

My mom's house had been in the eye of Hurricane Irma, and I went by to do some clean-up for her. There was a giant cactus that, prior to the hurricane, was ten feet tall, beautiful, and enormous. After the hurricane, it was broken and scattered all over the yard. As I cleaned it up, I was struck by how such a big, beautiful plant could have such shallow, weak roots and grow well beyond its capacity to endure a big storm. Of course, this cactus was native to the deserts of Arizona, not South Florida, so its evolution hadn't prepared it for hurricanes.

As I cleaned up, I was in a vulnerable and raw place. At this point, I was deep into exploring my past, my emotions, and unpacking a giant box of personal stuff, but I didn't have any real idea of

what to do with it all. My experience in the chasm of deep transformation is that it gets extremely dark, beyond confusing, and
frighteningly deep at times, especially in the early days. Sometimes, it felt like I had unleashed my own Pandora's Box.

The idea of just being with it and, even more so, leaning into it
was introduced to me by my coach, Stew. Occasionally, during
our sessions, I would be down or struggling. My instinct was
that being down was "wrong," and I wanted to know how I might
"snap out of it." He would ask me, "What if you just be with it?"
My initial reaction was, "Why the hell would I do that?" I was a
master of just ignoring it and moving on. All too often, I found
myself asking, *Why can't I just be happy all the time?*

Over time, I've come to appreciate that I need to embrace my
current situation exactly the way it is and feel it fully. Don't get
me wrong, I am not suggesting wallowing in self-pity, shame, or
blame, but I've found that I need to lean in and experience the full
spectrum of my current situation—the feelings and the thoughts.

To just be with it allows me time to acknowledge what's going
on inside me. It permits me to feel whatever I feel and not try
and convince myself that I shouldn't. This is a foundation to
living authentically and being whole. I've found that just being
with myself and my current situation has brought me profound
insights into what's going on within me and often opens the door
to even deeper knowing. It often allows me to let something go
after I've truly been with it.

Next time you find yourself having a bad day or in an uncomfortable situation, try just being with it. Be curious about the lessons
the situation is offering you. Be with it until you can say you're
done with it.

Another framework that I like to use is the "rule of thirds." In line with normal mathematical distributions, you can often split things up into thirds. Emotionally, there is a slice for feeling pleasant, average, and unpleasant. While I find that I spend more and more time in pleasant emotions, I fully embrace whatever my emotions are signaling to me. Once again, the key is that I am paying attention to them, not letting them blindly run my show.

This cactus reminded me of my current situation. I'd taken a beating in the recent "storms," and the carnage was messy. Was this my life once again? How many more times could I do this?

On some of the carnage, there were small cactus buds. *Hope for the future,* I thought. As the morning progressed, I continued to stop and look at the pieces and parts of this beautiful plant that I was piling up along the road in the front yard awaiting their removal. I knew this experience was a lesson presented to me. Instead of ignoring the signs, as I might have in the past, I took note. Before finishing, I took a few of the small buds off of the cactus and put them in a plastic bag to take home. One sits behind my desk on the windowsill today. It grows slowly with a solid root system and reminds me that flourishing is only possible with roots that can truly support me, even in the perfect storms. It also reminds me that a cactus isn't built for a big hurricane, period. It enjoys the tranquil and stormless environment of my office. It's really important not to confuse the two ideas.

That evening I went out for a drink. I was hanging on to what I always did and felt like I should grab one more "fix." You know, like the night before you start a new diet and you eat everything you promise yourself you won't eat tomorrow. The "last meal." I guess I figured I would have a little binge before I went straight.

It actually didn't turn out to be much of a binge, but once again, I noted the habit.

In the morning, I worked out and packed up. I was committed on a much higher level. A decade or so ago, I thought $49 was a lot to invest in something that might change my life. At this point, money wasn't going to get in the way of my transformation. *What good is money if I'm not fully alive and truly enjoying my journey?*

As I drove across Alligator Alley in South Florida, toward my walk on red hot coals, I had the convertible top down and some of my favorite songs playing on the radio. It felt like I was heading in the right direction. I knew this was exactly where I was supposed to be.

The following morning, I found a chair toward the back in the main ballroom at the Palm Beach Convention center with more than 5,000 other people. It was fairly calm, and I was comparing notes with people around me on how we ended up here. Many people said that someone else talked them into attending. After a while, someone announced, "Dancers on stage," and the energy in the crowd grew quickly. This energy and phrase would become familiar, but the first time, I was extremely confused. In a few minutes, the whole room was jacked up and dancing, the music was booming, and my whole body was vibrating along with the floor. It continued to escalate, and by the time Tony Robbins came on stage, the energy in the room was sheer pandemonium. While I was still pretty cautious at this point, you would have to be dead inside to not be at least a little excited. When things settled down a bit, I joked with the guy next to me, "Holy shit, what did I get myself into here?" He nodded and shrugged his shoulders in agreement.

It didn't take long before I was riveted to Tony and his message. He had a few interventions with people, and at some point, in each conversation, I thought, *There is no way this is going to end well.* But by the end of each interaction, each person seemed to realize a significant insight into their story, maybe a break-through. I was in the right place.

By that evening, I was dancing and jumping on my chair with the crowd. As some would joke, I drank the Kool-Aid. Late in the evening, I headed out behind the convention center barefoot and proceeded to walk twenty feet or so on the thin ashes that covered red hot coals. While I understood the science of why this works, it was still a real leap of faith. After my walk, I went back to my hotel room, and I knew I had found my crowd for this part of my quest. Yes, there were some hot spots on the bottom of my feet. But what was a little tenderness in the name of progress?

The following morning, I joined Tony's Platinum Partnership, year-long access to all Tony Robbins' events, including exclusive events. This cost me more money than anything I had ever purchased in my lifetime, except for my house. I often laugh to myself that I once hesitated to spend $49 on a DVD. I realized that my dark night had provided a once-in-a-lifetime opening and decided that the finan-cial commitment would keep me fully engaged for at least a year. I wrote a check and continued on my journey.

One idea Tony presented that resonated deeply with me was the idea of a primary question. The concept is that we all have a primary question in life—a question that we frequently revert to. It didn't take me long to realize my primary question was, *What's wrong with this (my current situation)?*

What's wrong with this? or *What's missing?*

While it came easily, this truly shocked me.

I sat in my chair for quite a while, absorbing this. It was probably obvious to many people who knew me, but facing my truth stung. I didn't consider myself a negative person, but evidently, I was quite adept at self-deception.

I remember running through my life like the old spell checkers that you ran in early word-processing software. Things lit up all over the screen. With anything new in my life, I immediately focused on what was wrong with it: relationships, jobs, purchases—you name it. I saw the same pattern.

There was something deeply unpleasant about admitting that my core question was, *What's wrong with this?* It was unsettling, to say the least.

In the depth of my quest for enlightenment, I experienced many truly unpleasant moments, and some were downright painful. During these, I reminded myself, *What if you just be with it?* So, I sat with my core question and examined how it affected my life up until this point.

I was truly ready for deep change at this point in my journey, but first, I had to enlighten my ignorance. I needed to know what I didn't know and learn what I needed to learn before any real transformation could occur. Maybe the experience wouldn't have been so moving at any other point in my life, but I was fully open to the lessons.

As I think about this period in my quest, I'm still amazed that I had never really thought much about how I operated or what I believed. I'd virtually spent decades in school learning about things like the composition of an atom and the details of nuclear fission but never took a single class in how I operate.

What is your primary question? The real one you often go back to?

Tony also spoke to us about our emotional home. This is the place we revert to emotionally when things get difficult or over-whelming. At first, I gave this my standard reply: *I don't feel anything.* But I knew I couldn't regress to old habits and evolve at the same time. As we explored this idea, I realized that my emotional home was fear, frustration, and lack (another way of describing my feeling of a void). Once again, I let this seep into my being and didn't enjoy it all. As I sat there, I realized that it wasn't that I didn't feel anything. Frustration, fear, and lack dominated my feelings for so long that it seemed like I didn't feel anything. I was feeling; I just didn't regularly feel anything outside these unpleasant core emotions. It was more that I was stuck in an emotional rut than not actually feeling.

My primary question and emotional home lined up well. Consis-tently feel frustration, fear, and lack, and it's not surprising that your primary question will be, *What's wrong with this?* A solid recipe for a lifetime of discontent.

The idea of human needs was another revelation. My core human needs were certainty and achievement. From child-hood, I wanted things to be certain because uncertainty typi-cally didn't end well for me. Achievement dominated my life for decades. I was the classic human doing, running wide open to achieve the goal or the bank statement that would make everything all right inside. If I could just make the completely uncertain journey of life perfectly certain and achieve a bunch, then it would be a wrap! Or maybe in all my running around, I'd just run off the edge of a cliff, and that would be that.

As would be repeated many times along my journey, these revelations didn't solve anything. They did continue to enlighten my ignorance, expose my mostly dysfunctional operating system, and create an opening to the potential of something more empowering.

My dark night had opened me, and UPW was the perfect place for me to explore ideas and places in me that I wasn't even aware existed or dared to examine. It was a space where I found I could really open up and just explore myself with new ideas, deeply probing questions, and a high-energy environment that didn't allow me to wallow in my massive uncertainty.

On the last day of UPW, I was completely engaged in it all when Master Co came on stage. While I had experienced my dark night, I still didn't see myself as a spiritual person. My initial reaction to a "spiritual teacher" was skeptical, at best.

When I began my quest, I promised myself that I was all in—whatever my journey presented. Some things were easier for me to remain open to than others, but I had found that the things that seemed to present the most resistance were often the lessons I needed the most. It was as if the toughest gates to open led to the richest awakenings.

As I walked toward my chair, Master Co told us to close our eyes and put our hands out, palms up. I stopped in the middle of the main aisle and did just that. It got darker in the room, and some "spiritual" music was playing in the background. In seconds, I felt this very distinct tingling energy in the palms of my hands. It was as if someone had a little electric needle and was poking the palms of my hands, moving clockwise in a clear circular pattern. I even opened my eyes to see if someone was screwing with me because it felt that real, but there was no one there. After a while, Master Co instructed us to open our eyes and asked if anyone felt anything. Some people raised their hands, and the first person he called on said, "I felt tingling moving clockwise in my hands."

"Interesting," Master Co said, "let's try again," neither acknowledging nor denying the experience. Some nodding heads in front of me indicated they experienced the same thing I did.

As the lights went down again, I felt the same feeling, except this time it was counter-clockwise in both palms.

What's going on here? I asked myself. While my mind continued to question, there was a knowing deep inside me that didn't need any explanation. We are all one, a fully interconnected and collective energy, consciousness—everything. If you completely let go, you can feel the entire universe.

I returned to my seat, and we sat for meditation. I had tried to meditate a few times before with little success. Typically, I never went more than a few seconds before my thoughts took over and I got frustrated, so I never stuck with it long enough to make any real progress. After my tingling-hands experience, I was excited to try again.

Master Co got us started with some discussion and short practices. Before long, we were in a group meditation, and my mind quieted quickly, and I was deeply meditating. Really deep. In a deep state, I floated off into another plane. I was swimming and breathing underwater, surrounded by the most amazing fish and beautiful people and places. It was as if everything I found beautiful in the world was now underwater, and we were all swimming and floating in this crystal-clear water. It was like an amazing psychedelic trip, except I was sitting in a metal chair in a room with 5,000 people as sober and clean as ever. The experience was so good that I never wanted to exit that euphoria. When Master Co began to call us back, I protested internally. *Why would I ever want to leave this place?* As my friends and I compared notes, some also had a deep experience, and many others, nothing at all. I said, "If I could bottle that experience and sell it, I would be an instant billionaire." While the spiritual and energetic gate had opened for me and I had passed through it beautifully, my mind was still hanging on to the idea of escape. As my journey evolved, these distinctions became clearer and clearer.

After four days, I was physically exhausted, riding on a cloud of euphoric possibility, and probably delusional as to what it all meant. The beauty of a peak experience like UPW is that it enlightened some of my ignorance and opened me to possibilities that my imagination had never considered. It felt like someone gave me permission to live, and while I didn't realize it at the time, I was learning to give myself permission. My excitement got a little ahead of itself or maybe like a thousand miles ahead of itself. With such an adrenaline rush and new experiences and realizations, it was easy to think I solved my problems or healed, and now I could get on with life. But my quest was only beginning, as I was just starting to learn what I didn't know and didn't fully understand; that knowing didn't mean realization or transformation.

The week after leaving my first Tony Robbins event, the high faded some, and there was a letdown for sure. The beauty was that I was heading back to Date with Destiny (DWD), another Tony Robbins event, in a few weeks in Ft. Lauderdale. If you want a glimpse of the event, watch *I Am Not Your Guru*, a Netflix documentary of the event a few years before I attended.

One of the great parts of being in the Platinum Partnership group is the incredible people you meet and the different topics you get to discuss. In the weeks and months between events, I began consuming everything I could from other sources. I listened to books non-stop and read at least one physical book all the time. If I was doing laundry, driving, or walking, I listened to some suggested material or something I found. It astonished me what was available and how deeply people had thought about self-improvement, health, and aligning yourself with your soul. It surprised me that that the questions I had been asking myself had been asked by people as long as humans have roamed the earth.

In December 2017, I headed to DWD, feeling excited to take the next deep dive into my authentic self. And this one turned out to be a really deep dive. At this point, I knew what to expect and was completely into it. "Dancers on stage" boomed over the speakers, and the room came alive. We were all eager for Tony to take the stage. We paired up with a partner at DWD, and it was a high-energy combination of teachings, group work, and individual work. The goal was to go deeper than you had ever been and figure out what was holding you back from living more fully.

I was jacked up at this point and would often get on my chair and dance, fully embracing the experience. This wasn't my normal quiet guy thing, but that playful kid came out in full force. The great part was the crowd was there with me.

Interventions are a key part of Tony's events. This is where he calls on people, and most often, the simple thing you think you're going to share turns out to be a thirty-minute or hour-long intervention into the depth of your being. The first few times I witnessed this, I thought there was no way Tony was pulling these things out in such a short time. And yet, every single time, before the intervention was over, the person's dam gave way, and they had an amazing revelation. Many of the stories are beyond heartwrenching.

A few days into the event, there had been several interventions that were really deep. Tony deeply engaged with one woman, but she continued to resist any meaningful breakthrough. Every time it seemed close, she would run for cover, and finally, her resistance forced Tony to bring the session to a close without clarity. I was feeling frustrated that she wasn't able to embrace her resistance and let go. Of course, it was a shadow of my own situation.

"Any guys want to share?" Tony asked as he walked toward the front of the room. My hand went up instantly. Something deep inside me pushed my hand up, and it shocked me as much as it would shock anyone who knew me at the time.

If you ever had a moment when you did something without your mind understanding how or why, you will understand what happened to me. When you raise your hand at this event, you are fully committing to whatever happens. It's like when you sit down into the Triple Dragon Death Spiral Roller Coaster, and the big metal shoulder restraint comes down and squashes your lungs to remind you that you have now committed to a ride that defies all logical reasoning. I was sitting about ten rows from the stage, looking at the screen with my hand up, when Tony pointed to me and asked, "What's your name, and where you from?"

Immediately, I panicked. I thought about saying, *No, you don't understand. I didn't really mean to raise my hand. I'll just sit back down.* But the coaster had just pulled out, and off we went.

During the last intervention, I felt the woman's hesitation to let go of what was holding her back. I felt a tension in me that I shared with her but honestly had no real idea what was going on with me or what I was going to say.

I started to tell Tony my story, and the words just poured out from somewhere inside me: my crash, prison, hiding my past, and the stress of living what felt like a life of dishonesty. Here I was, in a room of 5,000 people, most of whom I had never met, revealing the shameful, secret details of my life. The details I had decided to hide for the rest of my life when I left Florida years ago. The details even most of my friends and colleagues didn't know. But in this room, I gave my whole truth. I don't know how long the intervention lasted, but it was one of the most intense experiences of my life. The fear I felt that anyone who knew my story would be repulsed by what I did and by me played on the jumbotron for everyone to see, which at the time felt like the whole world. Tony was amazing and led me through it without making me feel any regret for baring my soul to strangers.

At one point, I moved out to the main aisle, and we were talking face-to-face. I remember looking up at the screen occasionally, and it felt like the whole thing wasn't even real, but it was so real. As we wrapped up, Tony gave me a hug that was so surprisingly sincere. I mean, this famous guy who seems bigger than life connected with me in a way that shattered much more than my story; it fundamentally changed me. It was like the hug I always wanted from my dad but never got. I don't know if my dad's spirit was there too, but that hug opened up—and, at the same time, filled up—a void in me that I had carried for decades.

When I sat back down, I felt like a giant boulder I'd been carrying for the past thirty years of life had been lifted off me. I was drained, relieved, and fulfilled in ways I'd never experienced.

Almost immediately afterward, someone from Tony's staff came with a release for me to sign, allowing them to use the content. *Holy shit. What did I just do?* The euphoria of the previous moment was instantly replaced by fear.

You see, my son was twelve years old at the time, and I hadn't broached the subject with him either. I didn't want him to hear about his dad's story from anyone other than me. I was quite aware that people were recording this and didn't want it to pop up on social media before telling him. I agreed to a release in ninety days and left it at that.

For the remainder of the event, a number of people came up to me and thanked me for sharing. They told me how it inspired them. I got an email from a woman who lost her daughter in a drunk driving accident and told me how my story helped her resolve some lingering issues she was suffering from. The attendees at the event were beyond amazing, and I couldn't have felt more accepted. My group and group leader were super supportive, and I am friends with a number of them today. I had faced my biggest fear, shared my story openly, opened another curtain, and exposed more of my framework.

One evening, we did an exercise on freedom. For any convict, freedom is a very welcomed concept. Tony played the freedom speech from the movie *Braveheart* with Mel Gibson. That got the men fired up, feeling something deep inside. We did some different exercises with partners, and at one point, my partner took my hand and put it on her heart. She said, "Feel that!" It felt like her heart was about to explode out of her chest.

In the movie, Mel Gibson asks the Scottish Army, "What will you do with your freedom?" I've watched the scene many times because it presents a foundational message for a truly authentic journey.

As a man who has fully felt the tyranny of a struggling father; the pure restraint of chains, shackles, and cuffs; confinement in one of the tougher maximum-security prisons in the world; and more mental prisons than I can count, I often ask myself, *What will you do with your freedom?*

You see, there is no freedom that you can grant a person if they are imprisoned in their own being. You can only find the keys to that gate after fully owning yourself and doing the often-difficult work of truly freeing your soul and truly living your soul, your truth. The experience with Tony was amazing and opened a gate to explore true freedom and what it meant for me. It gave me a glimpse of the true freedom I would someday realize.

My next key to freedom, I realized, might be the hardest moment of my life. I had to tell Collin about my past. I needed my son to know the truth to move forward on my journey toward greater freedom.

So, in late December 2017, a few weeks after DWD, Collin and I were driving to Florida for Christmas. I hadn't told him about my past yet, and driving along I-95 felt like the right time.

"I need to talk to you about something really important to me and will need your full attention. Is now a good time?" I asked. He put down what he was doing and replied affirmatively.

I spent the next thirty minutes or so telling him the whole story: from the night of the crash to deciding to tell a room of over 5,000 people a few weeks earlier. He sat listening intently for the entire time.

When I finished, I asked him, "You okay?"

He nodded quietly and then said, "You know, Dad, this doesn't change anything between us. I love you."

As the tears slowly trickled down my cheeks, I was speechless. If I had been scripting the movie, I might have rejected that phrase because I would have thought, *What twelve-year-old is going to say that? No one will believe it.* But my twelve-year-old son said it. He fully accepted his dad, without reservation, even after learning I caused a car crash that killed two people, resulting in years spent in prison and a good part of my life running from and hiding it.

When he said that, I was overwhelmed with a feeling of relief and filled with immense pride. I couldn't have been prouder of him.

Since the crash, I have always dreaded telling anyone. My primary fear of rejection always shifts into high gear. I imagine the person will see me as the monster I've so often seen in myself. Telling Collin wasn't just telling my only child. It was telling my young son something that could dramatically affect him personally and change our relationship forever. The stories I played out in my head before this conversation could fill at least a few bookshelves.

As we continued our drive, we talked about what he was thinking and feeling. He asked a few questions about what it was like and how it felt, and I answered everything honestly.

On our way to southwest Florida, we drove through Starke, Florida, and I asked him if he wanted to see where I had been incarcerated. He replied, "Yes."

As we drove under the arch that reads "Welcome to Florida State Prison" on the afternoon of Christmas Eve, 2017, memories flooded back. We pulled into the parking lot and sat. "This is it," is all I said. A few visitors came through the visitor's center doors and returned to their cars after their holiday visits. Memories of Christmas in prison are some of my saddest. The fences were everywhere, the razor wire sparkled in the afternoon sun, and gun towers loomed. A voice in my head kept telling me to leave before they threw me back in. Collin asked a few questions, and after a bit, he said he was ready to go.

As we pulled out, he said, "Dad, you know what? You're a fucking badass!" And we both laughed. It was the tense kind of laugh that eases the tension of everything swirling around inside you.

From time to time, Collin will ask me about various aspects of the accident and more so about prison, and we'll discuss it. Sometimes I'll use it as an example of life's struggles. When he comments about something I did as a young man in an attempt to justify his thoughts or actions, I'll usually say, "And I ended up in Florida State Prison doing time with Ted, so I'm not sure that's a good benchmark."

By January 2018, riding the high off of the Tony Robbins' events and the momentous drive with Collin, I was obsessed with exploring new avenues of personal development, spirituality, and transformation. If I wasn't reading it, listening to it, writing about it, or attending it, I was probably sleeping.

The action I was taking to enlighten my ignorance and learn about myself was massively opening my being, and I noticed some real changes, the first signs of real transformation. I was getting better at realizing my emotions and labeling them quickly. My body was getting healthier, and my mind, sharper. It was also a time of sheer chaos. It was like being in the middle of a complete remodel on an old house, and I was all over the place. There was stuff everywhere, and it wasn't entirely clear that it would all get back together and work well. At this point, I fully committed, and there was no turning back. I tore the curtains wide open and was fully engaged in the work.

One thing I struggled with fairly often was the feeling that I was in some way slow or just plain stupid as I continued to reveal the breadth of my ignorance. Fairly often, I would think, *How did I miss this or that all these years?* I'd look back at some event or relationship I struggled with and think, *Holy shit, how was that not obvious?* I didn't dwell here to beat myself up, but it was another aspect of the journey that I felt and worked with. I believe revisiting past events is extremely useful if you have some new tools to extract a greater lesson from the experience.

I'd come to realize that I hadn't always seized the moment in my life. My propensity to look for whatever was wrong in any given situation made it difficult to be spontaneous, especially in positive ways. I decided to exercise that muscle a bit. The Patriots were on their way to the Superbowl, and I surprised Collin with tickets to Minneapolis to see the game. The night before the big game, we attended a Dave Matthews concert—his first and my tenth. We excitedly watched the game, and in the end, the Pats lost. As a father, and especially considering the past month of revealing my past and what he had adsorbed, I wanted nothing more than to experience the perfect weekend that included a Tom-Brady last-minute comeback. I delivered, but the Pats didn't. There are moments as a parent when you wish you could control an outcome that's beyond control, and this was one of them. Regardless of the game's outcome, I'll always remember standing next to Collin at the concert and in the stands, watching a legend play in the Superbowl. I'll remember sitting at the pizza place after the game eating a great pizza, just soaking in the richness of the experience with him. Memories like that contribute to the wealth of my soul. Seizing the moment made it possible.

CONNECTING
THE DOTS

"You can't connect the dots looking forward: you can only connect them looking backwards. So, you have to trust the dots will somehow connect in the future."

—Steve Jobs

THE TRUE MEANING OF MANY OF THE PROFOUND MOMENTS IN my life, the dots, didn't come to light for years. Looking back, it's amazing how the dots connected. To truly surrender to the flow of life, you have to trust that the dots will connect. To truly experience life, you have to jump into a lot of dots.

A few years ago, a packaging supplier brought a new associate to my manufacturing plant. We were working on how to package our latest product. As we evaluated different solutions, they asked me about my business journey, and I told the tale of some of my pivotal moments: How I decided to start a company in the depth of a recession, made up a name that meant something to me, and moved across the country with nothing more than a vague idea. That I was just about out of money when I got a call out of the blue right before Christmas. Then, a few years later, I was locked up in a complex legal battle and amazingly threaded a needle out. The chemical plant I stood up in less than a month from scratch. How one of the biggest companies in the world adopted one of SAPREX's products. Patents granted around the world. People who appeared when I needed them most. Breakthroughs that happened at the wildest times. Insane hours, etc. At some point, I stopped and just stood there in silence. It was the first time I had stopped to appreciate how magnificently the dots had connected.

The new associate asked me, "How did you know what to do?"

"I guess I just trusted that what was presented to me was what I needed and jumped in, even when it didn't seem to make any sense in the moment," I said.

There have been so many meaningful moments along my journey. Part of my transformation has been to be fully present and embrace and truly appreciate the little and big moments in my life. One of the things I most appreciate is how the dots in my life have connected. Like a little boy smiling in excitement as the picture began to appear on a connect-the-dot drawing page of a coloring book, I'm amazed at just how beautifully the dots have connected. Here are a few meaningful "dots" that I haven't discussed elsewhere in the book. Most of them continue to get richer as their impact on my journey deepens.

THE BOX OF ACHIEVEMENT

It arrived via UPS. It was a small box from *INC Magazine*.

Once a year, *INC Magazine* presents the INC 500, the 500 fastest-growing private companies in America. I had long imagined how cool it would be to grow a company to be on this list. It was just a fantasy I never seriously thought I would ever realize.

I applied to *INC* in the spring and supplied SAPREX's certified financials. One of their writers contacted me about a feature article, but it never materialized. I stood at the desk and opened the box in silence. As soon as I opened the box, I would know whether SAPREX made the top 500 companies and, if so, what place. I was flooded with emotion. Excitement for the recognition. Overwhelm for the price I'd paid to get the company to this point. Acceptance that my pursuit of achievement almost consumed me.

As I opened the box, SAPREX was #324 on the 2018 INC 500 List.

The emotions of long hours, struggles, and persistence welled up inside me. I was overwhelmed with appreciation. It was a beautiful moment of recognition, one with roots much bigger than growing a company. It was a complex connect-the-dot drawing that got me here, and there were literally hundreds of dots that had connected to paint this picture.

While I have achieved quite a bit in my life, I never really felt like I belonged, especially on a big stage. As I stood there with the box in front of me, I just leaned into the moment. I had built a company that was the 324th fasting-growing private company in America. This was a success, and for the first time in my professional life, I was able to enjoy it for what it was. It didn't complete me or fill some void, but it was a recognition for a job well done. A recognition for the perseverance and commitment it took to get there. It was a drawing of many, many dots. I no longer needed this, but I enjoyed it. The wholeness of it all.

It was a long way from my Bob's Body Shop business plan conceived in the confines of LCI many years ago. I might even be able to call myself a legit entrepreneur now. Or maybe that's still a bit too much.

CREATURE

In my quest for development, I was recommended and read *Untethered Soul*. I fell in love with Michael Singer's words and wanted more. I picked up *The Surrender Experiment* next. In Chapter 31, titled "Metamorphosis of a Creature," Michael speaks about meeting and working with David Clark, a.k.a. "Creature." Creature was a leader of the Outlaw Biker Club that Michael meditated with for years before Creature was transferred to another prison, and Michael lost touch with him.

In that moment, my world stopped. I knew exactly where Creature went.

The State sent Creature to LCI, where he looked out for a young kid doing twelve years for manslaughter. He was the same guy who told my mom in the visitor's center that day, "Mama, it's going to be okay."

I had to read this chapter a few times. I was in utter shock as the picture of my journey jumped from the pages of my coloring book. It seemed implausible that Michael worked with Creature and that one of the toughest guys I met in prison became a devout meditator. Implausible that Michael's work with Creature had touched me many years before and likely made my stay in prison easier. It was one of those moments where you connect the dots looking back, and the real picture reveals a wildly deeper story. It's one of those moments when life's randomness doesn't seem so random.

Michael and I touched base after I read his book, and I let him know where Creature ended up and how he looked out for me at LCI. I thanked him for his work because it likely changed the very outcome of my life. It's a constant reminder of the subtle strength of our impact. That a seemingly small act might have a generational impact. It's a constant reminder that no matter where we find ourselves, we can have a positive impact if we do our work and leave the gate open.

VARANASI, INDIA

Manjit was sitting behind a table in the courtyard of a mission built by Mother Teresa. It was a quiet place, especially after walking through the noisy streets of Varanasi. The sun was shining, and I was enjoying the serenity. The entire courtyard surged with the energy of a deeply magical place—although, to the plain eye, it was a mission filled with people without many options.

It was clear that Manjit had impaired vision by the way his eyes looked off toward nowhere in particular. A small radio sat on the table in front of him, the kind that you used to buy for $9.99 at Walmart with the chrome metal antenna. He was listening to some music quietly. He had a sense of peace, and I was drawn to it. There was no doubt that we found ourselves in the same place to connect.

I sat next to him, but he didn't look at me. He was quite shy. I closed my eyes and quieted my mind to just be fully present. I just wanted to be there with him. We didn't need to talk to communicate. In time, he turned his head and looked at me. We were communicating. He didn't speak English, and I didn't speak Hindi. He showed me his radio, and I smiled. We listened to the music together and enjoyed the sunshine. A friend traveling with me walked up to the table, and ironically, he could speak both languages.

"How did you get here?" I asked through my interpreter. As he told his story, he said that he had lost his home, wife, children, and all of his family. He was the only one left. His vision was 90 percent gone, and he struggled to see shadows.

I asked about the radio, and he smiled. He liked to listen to music. It was so simple. His smile was pure and deep. It was the smile you see on the cover of *National Geographic*. It just draws you in and connects deeply. A soul smile.

He looked right at me as if he could see into my soul; in fact, we both knew he was already there. He knew why I had come and what I was searching for. A man with virtually no material possessions, no family, and seemingly nothing said, "I have lost my family, most of my vision, and my possessions. I came here, and when it's time, I am ready to go. I have everything I need."

I sat in silence and embraced one of the greatest gifts ever given to me. The connection that we shared in that moment spoke more than words ever could. Here was a man who appeared to have nothing, was blind and waiting to die, yet he was whole in the deepest sense. Truly at peace. I felt it in my soul and his.

I was a man of material wealth yet had spent the majority of my life tormented and empty. Spiritually broke. I was the man seeking what this man had become. His example was a beautiful gift to me. His example of purely being whole. Absolute surrender to life's impermanence and full appreciation of each moment for the gift it is. Fully accepting your journey and finding beauty in the pure simplicity of existence.

Manjit didn't need seminars, coaches, therapists, or books. He didn't need to undo fifty years of programming. He was at peace. He didn't feel the need to contribute something grand or live some extraordinary life. He wasn't asking anyone to fix his situation. He was simply being and fully appreciating the beautiful gift of being—appreciating his journey.

It blew me away. In that moment, a man who had no resources taught me what being whole meant. What it meant to fully appreciate your journey exactly the way it is, to appreciate the simplicity of having a place to lay your head and a meal. What an amazing gift he modeled. Our souls connected, and I realized why I traveled around the world to sit with a man I didn't know so that he could teach me about the true meaning of life and wholeness.

It was Mother Teresa's work that put the home there, which allowed that man to be sitting there on that day. A gift from the soul of the universe. Another dot connected.

All I have ever really wanted is to be at peace. Not worried about this or that, not planning the next thing, not worried about what he or she thinks, not seeking, not needing, not blaming, not grabbing, not doing, but just *being*. Being at peace with this very moment. Being at peace with me. At that little table, in a quiet courtyard, I was presented with that glorious lesson.

After we spent a good bit of time together, I spent some time in the kitchen that morning with the missionaries. They were an amazing group making lunch, hand-rolling bread, and making an Indian dish. One of the missionaries I spoke with was an American who had been around the world and helped many. She said, "This is the poorest material place I've ever served, but spiritually, the richest." I felt exactly that.

I received a lesson in truly connecting with my soul that day. A true connection with your soul is to be at peace with who you are, where you are, with what you have. To be able to let all of life's possessions and belongings go and embrace life's impermanence. To find peace in just being. Being in the moment and appreciating it for what it is. This is truly connecting with one's soul, our soul.

I'd traveled to Varanasi, India, and the Ganges River to experience a more spiritual way of life, a life different from our own. A world where what we call poverty is rampant, but poverty of the soul (so rampant in our world) was a stranger. I'd found exactly what we came for.

BLUE RIDGE MOUNTAINS, NC

One of my spiritual teachers suggested I build a drum and maybe participate in drum sessions. I found a shaman practicing in the mountains of North Carolina and arranged to spend the day with her. After several conversations, she said she would select an animal skin for us to build a drum in an ancient shamanic ceremony. She added that, if called to, we would conduct a soul retrieval ceremony.

On my drive up to her place, I was open and going way beyond the limits of my previous versions of being. At any point earlier in my life, I would have thought this entire adventure was more than a bit "crazy."

As we settled in, she informed me that she felt the elk connected with my strength, courage, and perseverance on my journey. With that, she had selected an elk skin to build my drum. As I lay with my eyes closed, in the trance of the ceremony, she lay the wet skin of the animal on my bare chest so that we could establish a meaningful connection. It was essential to the ritual that I feel the animal's spirit and allow it to connect with mine. As she presided over the ceremony, I remained quiet, connected, and just let the experience unfold.

In the depth of connection, the vision of the animal, of guides, and of legacy came clear. No words were spoken, but it was a deep journey. A journey way beyond the five senses.

After the ceremony, I built my drum by stretching the skin and rhythmically wrapping the cord through the skin and around the frame. Embracing this ancient ritual and truly being present with the experience connected me with something even more primal within me.

In the afternoon, she conducted a shamanic soul retrieval ceremony that was deeply moving for me. She felt the spirit of the elk within me and guided me to retrieve the lost portions of my soul. I felt my guides, and they journeyed with me. During the soul retrieval, I opened to a connection of ancestral legacy, to a connection of generations before me and the universal connection we all share. During the experience, I realized my deep ties to all the souls who came before me to deliver me to this time and place. Not just my genetic ties, but my spiritual ties too. It opened me to my profound responsibility as a spiritual being. That my journey isn't an isolated experience in this moment, but a part of the continuous experience of the millennia before me and that which will come after me. It's not just about direct connections to my family and friends but the entirety of the universal ecosystem, the legacy that brought me here, and my contribution to the universal future.

This experience opened me to realize that my existence and life journey are part of a long and elaborate relay race. The baton passed to me; my responsibility is to train hard, run with everything I have on my journey, and pass the baton to the next runner effectively and elegantly. It's not to focus on the runners before and after me or those next to me or ahead of me, but to appreciate them and my contribution to the relay. To ensure that my contribution to our whole is always better than it was yesterday. To realize that contribution is related to all the races that came before me and will come after me. To routinely ask myself, *What can I contribute to us?*

At times, I interpreted the question of *What will my contribution in this lifetime be?* to an externally grandiose contribution. I realize that even at life's simplest forms, we are connected to all that live in our time and to all that have and will live. As Victor Frankl suggests in *Man's Search for Meaning,* our purpose is to be responsible for our journey, regardless of its scope. It's understanding and embracing that we all carry the baton of existence, and with that comes our personal responsibility to be better and do our part.

My drum has a special place in my office, and from time to time, I put the drum close to my chest, close my eyes, and strike it. The raw vibrations of the drum echo through my body and better connect me with my guides, our soul, and our journey. This reminds me of my connection to the universality of my being. I find this especially useful during busy and stressful times when I start to indulge in my ego and overemphasize the importance of my current situation. It helps me align to our universal journey and understand the significance of the baton I'm carrying on a much broader scale.

IN THE RING

In the dimly lit front room of Johnny Tocco's gym in Las Vegas, I stepped into the ring with Nonito Donaire. I was no boxer but was in the ring to work with a multi-world championship fighter to push myself physically and go deeper into myself. To maybe break through more deeply to my truth. In that moment in the ring, I went beyond physically exhausted and had to reach into the often-untapped potential within me to continue. When we finished, Nonito spoke about feeling the giant spirit of the bear within me rise as it took over my exhausted body to protect me.

In that moment, I realized a deeper connection to my soul and its capacity. It reinforced that the limits my mind often attempts to place on me aren't absolute, and my true capacity is way beyond them. In the ring with a World Champion, in a gym where Sonny Liston and Mike Tyson once trained, I consciously experienced this. It was an experience to remind me that I was capable of so much more than the immediate limitations of my thoughts or discomfort. That there was a deep warrior inside, and I must practice summoning it and working with it.

It reminds me of running my first marathon. Around mile twenty-two, I hit the "wall." The exhaustion and discomfort I felt screamed at me to stop. At one point, I remember seriously fighting the urge to lay down on the side of the road and take a nap. It was a battle of will between my mind and body. I pushed through and survived the experience, but now I know that I didn't dig nearly as deep as I was capable of in that moment on that course. David Goggins does a great job of explaining and exploring this in his book, *Can't Hurt Me*.

Along my journey, I've met people who I feel deeply, and sometimes, they, me. As Nonito and I spoke of the experience, he described exactly what I felt: a connection of spirit. Much like my experience with Master Co, it was a connection of soul and of spirit. A deep connection, transcending the five human senses. A connection of our continuous energy and collective consciousness.

JULY 26, 2019:
TURNING FIFTY-FOUR

The morning began with the journal entry that opened this book. It was *the* day that began the real 365-day test of my transformation. Regardless of how many times I'd told myself or others had assured me that the legacy of generational suicide at fifty-four ended with my dad, I had to wake up on my fifty-fifth birthday to prove it. While I was in a great place, it didn't eliminate that nagging voice that had followed me since the revelation almost twenty years ago.

Nothing but 365 days of living would settle this once and for all—364 days and a wake-up.

In many ways, the curse of generational suicide was an extraordinary gift. It drove me to do my work and prepare. It drove me to leave nothing unexamined. It provided me the challenge to go deeper than I may have ever gone without it.

My dream of being fully naked in a crowded room represented the essence of embracing vulnerability, uncertainty, risk, and emotional exposure for me. As the curtains to my conceptual framework continue to be opened, I am deeply exposed to myself and to the universe. It requires me to consistently summon the courage to look into myself and confront any misalignment and internal conflict. It's not a singular event, but a committed journey to remain curious, examine me, and continue to expose and evolve. To tear down and rebuild any framework that doesn't best serve me and work to be better. To align more deeply with my soul. To align more deeply with our soul.

DHARMA SANGRA, CRESTONE, COLORADO

As I looked into her eyes from the fiercest warrior in me, she said, "Soften your heart. I want to feel your heart." I was confused, but she coached me. She didn't want me to lose the fierceness of my inner warrior but, rather, to learn to connect with my strength and my heart at the same time. I had never considered that I could be connected to my strength and have a soft heart at the same time.

In the early stages of my journey of self-discovery, I had learned to open to my emotions, my vulnerability, and my knowing. Initially, the openings were very compartmentalized. I was tough or vulnerable or connected, but not all at the same time. I was in the crawl phase of crawl-walk-run. The idea of being in all the spaces simultaneously was an expansion, and when she looked in my eyes and told me to soften my heart, I knew I was ready to expand.

Robert Moore's archetypes of a king, warrior, lover, and magician may shed some light. To be a true king, one must embrace them all and often be them all simultaneously. Embracing all that we are is essential for being whole and in full integrity with our soul.

So, I followed her lead. While maintaining my warrior, I opened my heart and connected with hers. I softened my eyes and relaxed my lips. She opened immediately, and I could see and feel it as she continued to open. It was truly amazing.

The woman? She was one of the practitioners at the event to help train and coach us. It was an amazing gift to experience this with someone who was so conscious and unattached to me. Someone who can give actionable feedback. An amazing gift for sure!

I spent five days with a small group of men at the Zen Center, participating in a Men's Intensive led by David Deida, Chris Sunyata, and John Wineland. For the majority of the event, we stayed in silence. The only words we spoke occurred when it was required of a practice or during a few meals when we were allowed to talk. We trained in masculine and feminine energy, being in meticulous integrity, and performed yogic practices. It was an incredibly deep experience that included time to wander into the mountain woods and just be alone.

Integrity is the state of being whole and undivided. It's fully embracing the depth of your soul and of our universal soul as a spiritual being. It's being fully present in your current human situation and in alignment with our soul. The Intensive expanded my understanding of this and how the practices of meditation, breathing, and my physical state all contribute to my degree of integrity in any moment. It opened me to realize that how I stand, walk, sit, and talk matter. I realized a much deeper being during the event that I continue to practice and evolve.

Have you ever just sat quietly and been complete? From time to time, I'll just sit and be meticulously present. Hold good posture, sit still, and just be present. I'll settle into that and just let go. Not meditating, not focused on anything except meticulously being. Most often, my mind will just go blank, and I will be in perfect alignment and at peace. The thing I have always been seeking. If you see me sitting in these moments, you may think I'm lost. Actually, I am perfectly found.

The simple task of eating a meal was different during the event. We entered the dining room and ate our full meal in total silence. We paid particular attention to how we moved and our posture sitting in the chair. We looked at each other deeply and with true curiosity. Without words, I allowed myself to just feel the people around me. I took each bite, striving to be fully aware of my actions, the taste, texture, and smell of the food.

Try eating a meal in total silence with others, fully present to everything about you and those you are eating with. Feel the texture, the taste, and your body's response to it all. Feel everyone around you. It's an amazing practice in expanding your true presence. In embracing what it means to be fully alive.

For me, the core of masculine energy is being fully present from my soul. I feel strong, knowing that what happens, I can and will handle it. The most significant shift for me is that I am not seeking to fix anyone but just be present for them. The feminine seems to consistently test the masculine core. In realizing this profound dynamic for myself, my interactions have become much clearer. The connection between the masculine and feminine is so much more than verbal. It's the masculine presence that the feminine seeks, not the words.

At one point, I asked David about my generational legacy. As much as I was growing and learning to create a new future for myself, the past still worried me. I was committed, but there was still a nagging little voice of uncertainty in me, seeking outside validation that I was going to be okay. His reply was basically, "I don't know what you'll do. Maybe genetics will dominate, and you'll kill yourself, maybe not." That's what I knew to be true, but not what I wanted to hear.

You rarely meet someone so solid in their core that they don't try to console you in this type of situation with something that they don't actually know. How often are we so authentically honest with others? Most people would have said something along the lines of "It's all going to be fine," when, in reality, they didn't know. In the moment after our conversation, I sat in the perfect uncertainty of my situation. I didn't know what was going to happen, nor did David. At that point, I was fully engaged in my self-realization and transformation, and I was doing my deep work. I would see my fifty-fifth birthday if I did and wouldn't if I didn't. It was a profound experience in accepting the absolute uncertainty of my human journey. I was doing my work, consistently improving my internal alignment and harmony and fully engaging with my human experience. That was what I could do. What I wanted from David was reassurance of the things that seemed out of my control. What I got was exactly what I needed: a lesson in showing up in full integrity.

What I've come to appreciate on my journey and moments like this is the fluidity of it all. I am constantly being better at being me, yet I am regularly tested and consistently realizing areas for improvement at the same time. I'm better at being me today than I was yesterday, and I will be better at being me tomorrow than I was today through my consciousness and dedicated work. Many days bring a new lesson and awareness of an opportunity for me to be better. It's not about healing, as I'm not injured or broken, and healing for me implies an endpoint. *We're done here.* True transcendence occurs when one's journey results in consistently becoming better at being more authentically you.

As I walked onto the plane on my way home, I was fully conscious and present. The stewardess looked at me, and we deeply connected. In my full consciousness, she opened with only a "Hello." I felt her, saw her face relax, and felt her heart and soul open. We spoke briefly during the flight, but each time we interacted there was a connection far deeper than words. As I exited the plane, we had the same experience, even more intense. There is beauty in these moments that needs no further pursuit. Just an appreciation of each other momentarily crossing paths on our journeys.

TAP

Soundly sleeping in the early morning hours of April 7, 2020, I felt a tap on my right shoulder. It was a very firm tap that woke me up. I rolled over to see what had awoken me in a bed I knew was empty—to a room I knew was empty. The tap was so clear, so distinct. I didn't remember a dream.

As I lay wide awake, a strong force settled over me. I immediately realized the "tap" was destiny calling. It was this reminder of what today was destined to be if I'd continued down the unconscious path I had been traveling. The tap reminded me that today could have been the day I terminated my contract with life.

In that moment, I felt the deep truth of our generational journey. The truth that we are responsible for our journey, and it's a much deeper journey than just me in this lifetime. My past generations come with me, and I am always leaving my imprint on the soul of our universal existence. My responsibility on this journey is to leave me and this universe better than when I was thrown into it. To improve my being and contribute a more powerful energy than I inherited. That is my responsibility as an energetic being. Laying there, I truly appreciated my journey and that my work was truly working.

In the past, I might have skipped right over this moment or celebrated in some external way. A "reward" to commemorate. This was a sign of grabbing for validation or escape for me. You may notice that I rarely use the word "celebrate" outside of birthdays and holidays. Celebrating is acknowledging a significant or happy day or event with a social gathering or enjoyable activity. Appreciation is to recognize the full worth of something. At this point in my journey, I had come to truly appreciate myself as a spiritual being having a profound human experience. I had come to truly embrace it all. In the appreciation and true embrace came a deep serenity that was life's ultimate gift for me. It was a deep feeling that I belonged exactly where I was on my journey.

Lying in bed that morning, I just enjoyed the deepest knowing that I did belong here. That I was exactly where I was supposed to be, doing what I could with what I had, and that I would leave this body for the generations that come after me better than when I was thrown into it.

DAILY PRACTICE

THE FOUNDATION OF MY ONGOING TRANSFORMATION IS rooted in my daily mind, body, and emotional practice. Just a few years ago, I would get up to an alarm clock after four or five hours of sleep, make a pot of coffee, jump into my projects in pursuit of achievement, and go till I collapsed. I'd spend my day mostly reacting to the world and very little, if any, time focused on taking care of me or exploring what's going on. The biggest change in life has been to integrate conscious practices focused on continuing my journey of self-discovery, self-realization, and self-development. My goal is to continue deepening my soul connection and better align and harmonize my body, mind, and emotions. To continue to awaken.

Ironically, I turned to some of the same fundamentals that worked for me years ago in prison: physical, mental, and emotional practices. It's crystal clear to me now that the bene-fits of transformation come with the obligation of actually being better today than I was yesterday, and my daily practice is the foundation of realizing that.

When the opportunity presents itself, I encourage others to begin and continue to develop a conscious daily practice that works for them. To help you develop your own daily practice, I'll share my current practice that continues to develop as I do.

These days, my daily routine starts with at least seven hours of sleep. I get in bed by 10:30 p.m. and awake at 6:00 a.m. seven days a week. I like to wake to a music alarm but am usually already waking up. A few deep breaths while I listen to some music let my body wake up gently. Entering into the day more peacefully than with a blaring alarm suits me much better.

While still in bed, I check my sleep tracking app and my continuous blood sugar monitor if I am wearing one. After getting out of bed, I check my vital signs (weight, blood pressure, and a few others) and drink the large glass of water I left on the counter before I went to bed. I then do some cold water therapy by jumping into a 56 degree Fahrenheit tank for five to ten minutes, wash up, make my bed, and meditate for twenty or thirty minutes. From there, I'll head to the kitchen, make a cup of coffee, and journal. Next, I'll walk and workout, maybe eat some breakfast, take a shower, and get out the door, typically around 8:00 a.m.

At this point, I'm in a great state as I move further into my day. If I don't get it all in, that's okay too. It's no longer something I *have* to do; it's something I want to do, so I rarely miss any of it. My practices throughout the day also help me stay energized and focused. Typically, I finish my day with some time for deep relaxation and recovery that typically includes a hot soak, lounging in my recliner, listening to a mellow genre of music, and reading a book. I'll often journal about appreciation, what went well during the day, and end with meditation before heading to sleep.

Integrating a solid framework of empowering daily practices that truly serve me is my foundation to living better each day.

HABITS

On top of my foundational practices, I regularly focus on improving my habits. These are habitual actions that I experiment with to better understand whether they enhance or detract from my life experience. The conscious practice of habit formation and modification reminds me that I am on a consistent journey to learn and grow. One of the first habits I experimented with was making my bed every morning.

Growing up, in the Navy, and in prison, making my bed was a requirement. It wasn't something I could choose to do or not do, and without that external responsibility, I left my bed unmade for the better part of the last twenty-five years. Believing I was just too busy for such trivial things, I told myself, *I'm just going to mess it up again tonight.*

A few years ago, I committed to making my bed every day for three months, no excuses.

For three months, I meticulously made my bed every day.

Today, I meticulously make my bed every morning, including placing the "fancy" decorative pillows in their respective places with the zippers down and corners aligned. If I start to head out of my bedroom without making my bed, there's a little "tug" in me indicating something is in conflict, and even if I'm running tight on time, I make my bed.

My initial reaction when I first heard the suggestion that making my bed was going to help me develop good habits was, "That's crap." But, after trying it for myself, I can tell you it's definitely not. It's my daily reminder of the power of habits. Modifying and creating new habits is pivotal to my transformation and living a life in integrity. Charles Duhigg's book *The Power of Habits* is a great place to start for more information on the life-changing force of consciously forming and modifying habits.

Our life is in many ways a reflection of our many habits. MIT Researchers determined that a habit consists of a cue, response, and reward. In the case of making my bed, the cue is walking out of the bathroom after washing up. My response is to make my bed, and my reward is the satisfaction of being in integrity with myself and my space. I no longer feel that I should or have to do it; I want to do it.

Habits can be empowering, neutral, or disempowering. Making my bed is a small empowering habit that helps start my day off with the win of being in integrity. A disempowering morning habit could be as follows: my alarm clock goes off (cue), and I pick up my phone to turn off the alarm, check my email (routine) and get engrossed in and reacting to the latest "stuff" (reward). This is disempowering for me, especially when it cuts into my workout or self-care. I'm not making proactive choices for my health or my soul in this habit. In fact, I'm mostly just reacting to what's happening around me but misaligned with my true being. So, I remain diligent in constantly improving my habits and often ask, *How can I better serve myself?*

Mastering the skills of habit identification, modification, and creation has been foundational to my transformation and evolution. After rarely making it for twenty-five years, I am still amazed at how I won't leave the bedroom without making my bed. I mean, it's truly wired into me. At first, it took discipline to make my bed and develop the habit. Now that it's ingrained in me, it doesn't require any discipline; the program runs on its own. It's a consistent reminder of the power of forming positive and empowering habits.

What new daily habit could you develop that would remind you of the power of habits in your life?

JOURNALING

I've been journaling on and off for the past twenty years. For the past four years, I have journaled virtually every day. Most days, I'll write at least a few pages, and some days, I write twenty or more following a thread that I need to express. It's become a daily "ritual" (a word I reserve for my most deeply meaningful habits).

I start each new entry with the day and date and end with a statement of love toward myself. Currently, I end each entry with "I love you, Bob. —ME," and I draw a heart. I always take a red pen and color the heart in. I started doing this years ago to develop the habit of expressing self-love. Over the years, women in my life would often write hearts in a card or note to me, and it felt loving for me, so I adopted it for my own daily self-expression of love. While this may not sound significant, I've found the small practices of self-love do reinforce.

Between those two bookmarks, I ask myself, *What am I feeling?*, *How am I doing?*, *How will I actually be better today than I was yesterday?*, and *What do I really appreciate in my life?* Then,

I elaborate as much as I need to. The habit of checking in with myself daily helps me better understand the natural rhythms of my life.

After my daily questions, I typically follow some thread of consciousness or specific practice I am working with. When I want to develop something meaningful to me, I practice every day. For example, each day I start with the question, *What are my rules?* and then proceed to write them from scratch, not copying yesterday's. Each day I began with a clean slate. After months of doing this, they typically flow well and are a good representation of my truth. Once they feel solid, I typically let them be for a period of time.

Journaling is a great activity to practice inquiry. It's where I often ask and ponder questions. I work with my thoughts, beliefs, emotions, and experiences. It's where I explore friction and harmony. It's where many of my breakthroughs have begun and especially where they have evolved. It's a safe place that truly helps me see through my own deception and gain much-needed clarity to further develop. For me, the tactile and visual stimulation of writing brings an added level of authenticity.

Journaling is a sacred activity for me. It's my daily thinking time. I prefer to "think" with a pen and paper. I have a specific type of book and pen I love to write with and almost always have my latest journal with me. I love to journal early in the morning before the sun comes up and the house is perfectly quiet with a freshly brewed cup of coffee. It's truly one of my favorite parts of my day. I easily slip into the flow and typically have to force myself to stop. I also pull out my journal when something strikes me or I want to remember something to explore.

I have a stack of full journals on my shelf that are a legacy of my journey.

For me, journaling is as foundational as meditation in being whole. It's where my feelings, thoughts, dreams, ideas, and just about everything else come together.

If you've never tried journaling or are not a regular journaler, I recommend that you give a journaling practice a try.

MEDITATION

My first experience with anything related to meditation was on the floor of the psychology trailer at LCI. Dr. Mauer suggested I listen to some relaxation tapes, which I did every week after our session. A half-hour of laying on the floor in a silent room without threat was heaven in the penitentiary. My favorite practice was to close my eyes and imagine that with each inhale the "blocks" of tension inside my body would be drawn into my breath, and then, with each exhale, I would blow them out. I still do this visualization today, especially if I am feeling stressed. I often do this as I lay in bed before sleep to clear the day from my being.

The biggest benefit of meditation training is that I have quieted the incessant chatter or self-talk that dominated my mind space for the majority of my life. For the first fifty years of my life, my mind was always busy thinking about this or that. Often most of these thoughts were ruminating about the past or worrying about the future. The only time I didn't have the chatter was when I got deeply engrossed in a project I was working on, especially one that challenged me. Today, the state of distraction-free work is often referred to as "flow" as originally popularized by Mihaly Csikszentmihalyi. One of the main reasons I spend so much of my time in projects is that I love to be in a flow state.

Through meditation training, I learned to quiet my mind completely, instantly, and in almost any situation. As I sit here deeply working on this book, I can stop, and my mind immediately goes silent. No thoughts.

It took me several years of daily practice to realize this monastic level of internal stillness.

Stillness is an amazing foundation for being truly present in the moment. When I smell a flower, I am fully engaged in the delicious aroma that excites my nose. I allow it to dance with my soul. When I kiss my lover, I am fully immersed in the smell, touch, and feel of her and openly give myself to the moment without the distraction of anything else, including analyzing what I'm doing or how it's being received.

I'd tried meditation a few times over the years. To be honest, it just didn't resonate with me. It was my introduction to Pranic Healing meditations with Master Co that opened the gate for me. Over the past few years, I've explored a number of other methods as well. The method isn't the point; the realization of quieting the mind and realizing stillness is.

It's important to acknowledge that we are often open to different habits and rituals at different times in our lives. Something that didn't work for you years ago may be just the thing you need now, in your current self and situation. One method may work better for you at some times than others. The key is to remain open and keep exploring. To ensure that I'm always growing and learning, I never completely write off a potential practice. Along my journey, I will need different tools and habits. The same is likely true for you.

Early in my meditation journey, Sage Robbins strongly suggested that the euphoria of meditation is not the point when I shared with excitement my meditation "trips." Meditation practices help us connect and quiet our minds, which are the foundation of present moment awareness, she told me. It took a few years for that message to fully resonate and develop with me. With much practice, it completely transformed my life. It's easy to let meditation be the end game. To become a "meditator." But for me, it's a foundational training that allows me to experience life more deeply, not the point of life.

Meditation is far from "new age." It appears to date back at least 7,000 years from indications of early cave drawings. I imagine that as soon as our minds evolved to allow consciousness, we began to struggle with realizing it. Mediation is one of the deepest learnings that was passed down for thousands of years, and my life wouldn't be nearly as rich without it.

Today, my meditation is uniquely my own. Over the past few years, I studied and adopted a number of techniques from various teachers. I have a mediation blanket and zafu that I sit cross-legged on in my bedroom. I am conscious of my posture. In honor of my beginning, I always start with a few deep "block" breaths to release any tensions. As I breathe in, I draw any tensions together in my breath, and then, as I deeply exhale the breath out of my mouth, I see and feel them released. It's like cleaning the palate of my being.

During one of my practices, I do a fire breath where I breathe in deeply and out shallowly for thirty or so breaths until I feel the satiation of oxygen. At this point, I hold my breath until my chest begins to naturally convulse. I stay with the convulsions, trusting that my body will tell me when I've had enough. At that point, I take one deep breath and hold it until a wave of relaxation comes over my body and let that sit for a bit. Afterward, I breathe out deeply until I cannot manage even the slightest additional exhale. Then, I inhale deeply through my nose and let that settle.

At this point, I tune in to each of my sensory functions, one at a time. I spend time noticing everything I physically feel, hear, see (with my eyes closed), smell, and taste. Then, I practice them all at once. From there, I practice alternate nostril breathing. At this point, I take a deep breath and settle into my core. I ask my soul, *What do you need to tell me?* and wait quietly for a reply. Some days, there is an answer and some days not. I keep myself open, fully accepting either. Finally, I open my palms upward and settle into quiet meditation. I've worked with breath-based meditation and other techniques, but today, I typically allow myself to just be monastically silent if I am in that space. If silence doesn't come easily, then I will follow my breath at the tip of my nose or focus on the flow of energy through me. I embrace what I need in the moment.

Meditation practice has massively expanded my being. It allows my mind to quiet, embrace stillness, and be more present in the moment. It's helped me better connect with myself and hear what my soul, body, mind, and emotions are telling me. It's helped me feel the subtleness of life's whispers. With this foundation, I can authentically be present in this moment and explore so many other experiences in life, including sights, sounds, smells, and tastes. I really can't adequately emphasize the positive impact it's had.

BODY

Taking great care of my body has many parallels to a plant. A plant needs healthy soil, sunlight, and water. It needs some clear space and not too much competition from other plants but actually thrives with a variety of other plants around. When it's strong with deep roots, it can thrive in harmony with all of nature, its ecosystem. When its ecosystem is strong, it can handle big storms and is highly resistant to disease and the attack of harmful insects. The strongest plants typically don't live indoors but live in harmony with a more challenging environment. A plant is a living, breathing organism that will quickly tell you how it's doing. With an optimal ecosystem, it thrives in wholeness. It won't fully flourish when things are off in the ecosystem, and it is often much more susceptible to outside attack. When things are really off, it wilts and may die. My body is similar in its ecosystem.

The more I continue to evolve, the more I realize just how deeply my body is an integral part of my overall ecosystem, including mind, emotions, and immunity, to name a few. I've often eaten for convenience, the momentary pleasure of taste, or grabbed for food to satisfy my boredom or frustration. I routinely drank and, at times, did drugs to escape my current reality. More often than not, I treated my body like a receptacle for anything and everything I decided to throw in it rather than an integral part of my ecosystem. For stretches, I neglected it entirely, and it wilted. Other times, I was obsessed with how it looked but rarely concerned with its inner working and true harmony, unless it wasn't working well. I may have looked good but wasn't in harmony and had weak roots. When it wasn't working well, it would get my attention, and I'd be better...until I wasn't.

As I struggled to build my company and was on the verge of a breakdown, my health rapidly declined. At 280 lb., I experienced all the side effects of an extremely unhealthy body. My blood pressure was skyrocketing, and I regularly bought bigger pants to fit into. Rather than face reality, I would rip the size tag out of each new pair, fully in denial of my bulging waistline. I was eating a lot of fast food, drinking way too much coffee, a few energy drinks a day, and sleeping as little as possible. I was one of those people who bragged about how little sleep I needed as I thought sleeping was a waste of my time. It was a recipe for physical, mental, and emotional turmoil, to say the least. Ultimately, it contributed to my total collapse.

Other times in my life, I was in great shape, eating well, lifting, stretching, and running regularly. I've run a marathon, a bunch of half marathons, and various 5k and 10k races, mostly in search of some magical body or state of "health." Subconsciously, it was another one of my projects geared at negotiating with the universe for some magic solution for fulfillment. Just like many of my well-intentioned pursuits, it didn't "fix" me. While I felt better during these stretches, I muscled my way into shape, and it lasted as long as my willpower did, which wasn't typically very long.

Today, I feel great much of the time and am very in tune with my body. I am consistently getting better at tuning in to my body, actually feeling and listening to it. I pay attention to how my body responds to what I eat and drink, how I sleep and exercise, and what's going on in my life. Instead of letting my mind or emotions dictate how I treat my body, I let my body lead the way. When I am in flow with my body, my mind is incredibly sharp, and I have a great deal of energy. The harmony feels amazing.

On my quest, I heard about fasting a few times. Those who tried it seemed to have positive things to say about it. After doing some research, I decided to try it for myself and have had amazing success. For more than a year, I water-only-fasted for thirty-six hours three times a week. I would eat Sunday night and again on Tuesday and Thursday, skipping eating entirely Monday, Wednesday, and Friday. Sometimes I would fast for three- to seven-day blocks. Of all the things I do, this one gets the most reaction from people. Typically, it's something like, "That's crazy!" or, "That's way too much. I am not doing that."

More and more, I realize that many ancient traditions were well-founded on experiential learning and often sounder than many of the ridiculous things we do today. People have fasted since there were people, primarily due to food scarcity and, for centuries, for health, religious, and political reasons. Our bodies have evolved to store fat and burn fat for fuel because the next opportunity to eat could be a long way off. The food abundance available to many people today is a very recent phenomena on an evolutionary timeframe and the reality is many of us eat way too much, way too often. Fasting lets our body exercise the actual function of using the fat we haul around with us for times of food scarcity.

Researches are rediscovering why we may need to fast. Fasting gets our body into fat-burning mode, and with that, many of our hormones activate, something they aren't required to do in an overfed state. When I fast, my thinking is clearer, my energy goes up, and I have a lot more time since I am not spending time preparing and eating meals. If you want more information on the benefits of fasting, I strongly recommend Dr. Jason Fung as a starting point.

I have found that a predominantly plant-based diet and meat from ethically-raised or wild animals is the diet that optimizes my being. I eat virtually no processed food, vegetable oils, or refined sugar. I predominately eat a whole food diet; if nature didn't make that actual thing, I don't eat it.

A few years ago, I started growing vegetables hydroponically and then organically in my own garden, which continues to expand. Managing a large organic garden provides me with much more than fresh produce. It's truly teaching me about system ecology and how truly amazing the whole system is, including my part in it. As I get better at cultivating the ecology of my garden, from the health of the soil to the types of plants, the legacy of seeds, and the bugs and weeds, I get better at embracing my ecosystem and our ecosystem. It also provides me with regular, natural exercise, daily fresh air, and some sunlight. If this idea interests you, a great place to start is *Farmacology* by Daphne Miller, MD.

These days, I eat much of my diet immediately after picking vegetables I have grown to full ripeness. I walk my garden virtually every day to keep in tune with my plants. Walking around and sampling different plants still amazes me. It's also deeply satisfying to see my teenage son's amazement at the depth of different flavors of fresh vegetables and spices or hear him genuinely compliment today's lettuce. One of my great pleasures is picking a vegetable and standing next to the plant, truly tasting and fully experiencing it immediately after picking it. If you want to eat something truly alive, try growing it.

Growing my own vegetables allows me to select the plants I grow and diligently care for them. It also allows me to eat seasonally as I predominately eat what's flourishing outside in my garden. I grow almost all of my plants from seeds that I am consciously sourcing. You can grow very different plants when you remove the need to ship and keep vegetables "fresh" for days or weeks. I think we all know that lettuce shouldn't still be "fresh" in the fridge two weeks after you bring it home.

It turns out that growing even a little bit of your own vegetables can have a much deeper and wholesome effect. It introduced me to the natural harmony of sun, soil, plants, animals, and me. It keeps me around people who are truly invested in their health and the health of our planet. It's also helped me tune into vegetables if I shop at a farmers' market or grocery store. These days I can pick up a vegetable and know if it's been well cared for and something I want to put in my body. Studies have shown that children and adults who grow vegetables eat more vegetables for their entire life.

Planting, tending, and eating from a garden with your kids may be something that influences them for life.

As much as possible, my meat and fish come from local farmers and fishermen I know, most of whom I have visited.

Bone broth made from scratch in my kitchen is another staple of my diet. Once again, I source bones, tendons, feet, and organs from local farmers. Every few weeks, I make a large pot of broth from a variety of animals. I freeze most of it in glass jars and drink the broth regularly.

What I eat and drink and the supplements I take are constantly evolving. My journey is to continue to refine and improve my energy, clarity, and wellness. I want to live better, longer, and do all I can to live beyond 125 years with great health.

Breathing is another area of my journey with my body that requires a full transformation. Yes, just regular breathing. It turns out we often breathe much too shallowly and much too often. Breathwork is another practice that dates back thousands of years. My optimal breath is a five-second inhale followed by a five-second exhale, all through the nose, starting from my lower abdomen. I practice this often. Driving, sitting at my desk, working, and working out are all activities where I focus on my breathing.

Some nights I sleep with my mouth taped shut, which some of my friends probably wish I would do during the day. This forces me to breathe through my nose all night. I notice that I sleep much better, and the restriction trains me to breathe through my nose while I'm awake. If this interests you, a great place to start is *BREATH* by James Nestor.

Like breathing, I have also done a lot of work on my sleep to serve my body better. I now block at least seven hours of sleep time for myself each night. The temperature of my bed is regulated and varies during the night to optimize my sleep phases through a water-cooled pad. I wear a sleep monitor and constantly correlate how I live and my sleep patterns, including how much deep, light, and REM sleep I get per night. What and when I eat and drink affect the quality of my sleep, so I pay attention to my eating habits to optimize my sleep. Sleeping better and longer has significantly improved my energy, thinking, moods, and cravings. *Why We Sleep* by Matthew Walker, PhD, is a great book about sleep.

My workouts include walking, running, lifting, and biking, mostly in my home gym or outside. At the very least, I make time for a twenty-minute workout that includes a rebounder plus my speed and heavy bags. I lift heavy weights and do high-intensity training at least three times a week. The goal is a variety of exercises and often real physical work in our manufacturing facility or garden. One of the things I love about my gardening is that I regularly use a rake, shovel, ax, hoe, and a handful of other tools. This keeps my body active and engaged in movements we've been doing as humans for centuries. While I love scheduled workouts, I go out of my way to move my body in natural work as well.

Virtually every day, I take my blood pressure and measure blood sugar and ketones. For stretches of time, I will use an app and track everything I eat, especially if I am making a change.

Recently I began working with a functional medicine doctor. We truly focus on whole health and include several deep and detailed tests to better understand how my body is working and aging. A real key is to correlate what I am doing and eating with how my body is quantifiably responding.

While I consistently seek to improve my health and fitness, I feel better than I have my entire life, and it keeps getting better. Much of what I have learned and applied in the past few years has completely changed my understanding and appreciation of my body and my ecosystem.

While you may not be ready for a full-body transformation, true harmony requires truly listening to and caring for your body and the whole ecosystem. The missing piece you're constantly distracted by may feel like it is solely an emotional or mental component, but your body is likely intertwined in it all. As you experiment with new practices, pay close attention to how your body feels, including your thoughts and emotions, not just how it looks or can be quantified. While emotional and mental transformations will be paramount in your overall transformation, remember that your body is an integrated part of your ecosystem.

MIND

My mind is clearer and sharper than it's ever been. Better physical health, better sleep, and eliminating the incessant chatter and stress in my being have all contributed. My mind now gets time to rest and is well fueled and regularly challenged. Considering I rarely slept more than five hours, ate like crap, and my mind constantly chattered on, it's a wonder I accomplished as much as I did.

If I were attending school today, I might be labeled ADD. Luckily for me, I've learned to embrace my incessant curiosity and deeply focus at times to channel it. When I am in flow, I am as focused as it gets. When I am not, I am wildly curious and typically have my hand in at least a few "jars." It's not always pretty, but it's me.

Taking care of my mind includes eating, not eating, sleeping, exercising, and meditating—and being very conscious of their impact. I used to push through things and now pay close attention to how my mind is working. A quick walk or a five-minute workout will often help me dial back in if my thinking is fading. A few deep breaths where I inhale clean focus and exhale the blocks of distraction work wonders. If I am engaged in deep thinking, I will often take a twenty-minute afternoon nap to balance my autonomic nervous system. That quick break, followed by a green tea or coffee with MCT oil, and the next few hours will be some of my best thinking of the day.

Training my mind also includes asking questions and investigating beliefs.

It wasn't obvious to me that the questions I asked myself were directly related to the quality of my life. This idea was first presented to me by Stu, later reinforced by Tony Robbins, and further solidified through several books on the subject.

At its simplest, I began the process of transforming my primary question from *What's wrong with this?* to *What can I appreciate about this?* The inconvenient truth is that realization rarely results in spontaneous transformation. While I knew that my sometimes-disempowering primary question wasn't always serving me, it's taken a consistent practice to shift to the more empowering question and takes ongoing practice to continue to strengthen it. For the past few years, I journaled about what I was truly grateful for most mornings, and in the evening, journaled about at least five things that went well that day. These consistent practices began to settle in, and I found myself more appreciative in more and more instances.

An important point is that *What's wrong with this?* isn't a bad question, and *What do I appreciate about this?* isn't a good question. They are just questions. For a while, I labeled *What's wrong with this?* as a bad question. In reality, it serves me well at times. *What do I appreciate?* also serves me well. Wholeness requires a breadth of questions.

As my questions were changing, my overall physical, mental, and spiritual state were as well. It is easy to ask, *What's wrong with this?* in a depressed state but much harder in a positive state. The state supports the question, and the question supports the state.

What we believe are those things we accept as true. It shocked me to learn that much of what we believe is false, some studies suggesting more than 50 percent of what we believe is false under normal circumstances and north of 90 percent under high stress. That means that a large portion of what I believe is false. But I believe it.

It turns out that we accept all kinds of things that are presented to us but don't research or evaluate them ourselves. "People are credulous creatures who find it very easy to believe and very difficult to doubt. In fact, believing is so easy, and perhaps so inevitable, that it may be more like involuntary comprehension than it is like rational assessment," according to Harvard psychologist Daniel Gilbert.

What's even better is we believe things that are untrue even after we are presented with solid evidence that they are untrue. *Huh?* It seems we are wired to favor efficiency over accuracy.

To further complicate this, much of what we believe is unconscious, and we never go back to check our premise.

One of my favorite questions is *What must I believe for that to be true?* followed by *Can I be certain that is true?*

Improving the quality of the questions I ask myself and constantly checking my beliefs are core to evolving my mind.

EMOTIONS

Having worked extensively to understand my emotions and truly embrace a wide range that I experience in any given time period, I continue to train my emotional muscles. During my meditation, I dedicate time to truly be with myself and ask myself, *What do you need to tell me?* I also start each morning journal session with, *What are you feeling?* I'll often look up new emotional words and use an app that helps me expand my emotional language.

Having been anchored in a mindset of fear, lack, and negativity for decades, it's important that I allocate time every day for appreciation. This includes mental and journal exercises. This regular training keeps me building my more empowering emotional grooves and muscles.

While I spent a large portion of my life stuck in a very narrow emotional window, I now experience and embrace a much broader range of emotions. My goal isn't to be happy all the time but to truly experience the full breadth of my emotions and what they are trying to tell me. For me, it's about being tuned into the full breadth of my human experience and how it feels.

The shift wildly enhanced the arena of being and the breadth of my experience. Just the simple pleasure of smiling, having a good laugh, or embracing my tears is truly a gift for me.

LIVING TO LEARN

*"A mind that is stretched by a new experience can never go
back to its old dimensions."*

—Oliver Wendell Holmes

SITTING AT MY KITCHEN COUNTER IN THE PERFECT SILENCE OF
the pre-dawn morning, I laid my pen down from journaling.
Slowly sipping the last of my morning coffee, I let my journal
entry fully settle with a deep breath of acceptance. No doubt,
I was deep in the chasm that separated my dark night and my
potential as a spiritual being on a beautiful human journey. I
was also feeling very unsure of where I was in my own transformation.

Where to from here? I asked myself.

The learnings and insights from a few years of diligent exploration since my dark night were like drinking from a fire hydrant. I

was drinking a lot, but much of it was flying by. I wasn't entirely sure I was getting the stuff I needed or if I'd even been exposed to that yet. During my week in Crestone, we were rarely allowed to talk, never allowed to take notes during sessions, and had no phones. *Take what you need and leave the rest* was the message from the experience, and it resonated deeply with me. It's irrelevant how many events I attend, how many books I read, how many notes I take or how many insightful things I post. It's great to have more knowledge and tools. Yet, all that matters is who I am genuinely being and becoming.

Take what you need and leave the rest, I said to myself.

When I came to a dark, dead-end, I was embarrassingly ignorant as to what was going on in my life, how to actually transform my being or if it was even possible. Immersing myself in everything that called to me was what I needed to exponentially enlighten my ignorance. The inconvenient truth is that I couldn't possibly absorb it all, never mind apply it all. Nor did I need to. Many things were similar at their core but presented differently. There were ideas that conflicted with others, and there were things that just didn't resonate with me. I needed to better understand who I was and how to simply be better at authentically being me.

What do I really need? I asked myself.

There were still many legacy beliefs and behaviors tagging along that were no longer serving me, and that confused me. From time to time, I would ask myself, *Where did that come from?* when I did something that seemed so much more consistent with the me of twenty years ago than that of my present moment.

What don't I need? I also asked myself.

It was clear to me that there was probably a lot more stuff that I still didn't know about myself than I did. I still needed to unpack that stuff, better understand it and work with it.

As I reflected on the first fifty years of my journey, it was clear that I often over-complicated life and that much of it was based on things that just weren't true. My personality was often unconsciously running a program based on a false story. Bad story in, bad story out. It was fascinating and terrifying to come to realize that all too often, I didn't know who I was, how or why I saw the world the way I did or why I did what I did.

That's just the way I am wouldn't cut it anymore.

I decided to take a break from massive consumption and focus on refining my understanding of what I need and don't need. To take what I truly need and authentically apply it. To focus on further enlightening my ignorance and transforming toward transcendence from a human blindly doing to an awakened spiritual being. One key to realizing the transformation required to exit my chasm appeared to be truly getting to know and understand myself better.

If you jump into the journey of self-discovery, self-realization, and transformation, you may come to this point as well. I found that this is a pivotal time when we can choose to fool ourselves that our transformation is over, we are "healed," or we can commit to go on in pursuit of an ever-deeper truth. In my experience, the only way to truly realize transcendence into a spiritual being is to go deeper, much deeper. There appears to be no limit to our depth and potential.

I share this with you, not so that you can adopt what worked for me. That wouldn't be authentic to you. I invite you to use these foundations to explore you, what works for you, and what aligns your being in truth and integrity. The key is to realize and authentically live your truth more deeply each day!

VISION

In the self-help world I immersed myself in, I'd been asked over and over again about my vision for the future. To be honest, I could never come up with anything that inspired me. I'd spent the last twenty-five years working hard. I'd earned a few college degrees, traveled the world, had money in the bank and accumulated some cool stuff. I'd loved, and I'd lost. I have a great son. A dream? A vision? Externally, I was focused on achieving something that validated me and hoping I would arrive in my very own Shangri-La one day. On the inside, I just wanted less struggle and more peace and harmony.

What do I really want? or *What do I really need?*

First, I needed to define what I meant by wants and needs, so I could answer as honestly as possible. To me, a want is a desire to possess or do something. In other words, things I wished for. On the other hand, a need is something that I require as an essential part of my life. It's pretty easy to confuse these ideas.

My dark dead-end and the reality of being a fifty-four-year-old with a generational legacy of suicide at fifty-four were a constant reminder to stay focused on what I need, not what I want.

I must become better at truly being me was what I knew I needed.

In the circles I was traveling in, I often felt like I was supposed to have some grand plan to save the world or something similarly grand. I came to fully accept that I had to save myself first. While my understanding of this concept continues to evolve, I realized that if my internal operating system was allowed to continue, I might not survive.

It didn't take long before I started asking a lot more questions.

"The quality of your life is determined by the quality of the questions you ask."

This is a well-known statement in personal development. I've found it to be true as a great question inspires me to go where I may not have gone without it. Over the past few years, I have asked and deeply thought about hundreds of life-probing questions. I've intently listened to others' questions about themselves and me. It's truly powerful when I do the work to authentically answer the questions.

The full power of the question is harnessed in realizing and fully embracing your truth. It's quite easy to ask a great question of yourself or others. It's a completely different experience when you actually want to know the answer, the sometimes painful and brutally honest answer. It gets really interesting when you ask and won't stop till you get to the root of your truth.

With that in mind, I expanded my core questions to help me seek the answers I needed to truly be better a being me. I asked myself:

- What do I really need?

- Why do I really need it?

- How could I get it?

- What will I do to get it?

- When?

Often an insight presents itself at the most unexpected time. I might be mowing the lawn and see a bird do something that leads me to an insight relating to something I have been thinking about for months.

I also started frequently asking myself, *What must I believe for that to be true?*

One morning, I was journaling and playing around with words. I've never been a vocabulary junkie, but I've realized that I don't fully understand the meaning of many words I routinely use and avoid a lot of words because I don't know what they mean. The exercise of looking them up helps deepen my understanding and my ability to communicate, at the very least, with myself.

I looked up *whole*. The definition read, "complete within itself."

I stopped writing and let that settle in. Whole. *That feels right*, I thought to myself. Complete within itself. If I am whole, then I am complete within myself.

What does "whole" mean for me? I asked.

Whole is knowing who I am and being in alignment with that. It means being fully engaged and fully experiencing life with minimal internal friction. It means my body, mind, emotions and spirit are in harmony and well aligned with my soul. It means being fully responsible for and accountable to me. It means I am doing my work and running the best leg of the universal relay I can.

It also means I wouldn't constantly be feeling a void, inadequate, cracked or broken. I wouldn't be grabbing for things to avoid my reality or chasing the next thing to "fulfill" me. I wouldn't be measuring myself against or living someone else's life; I'd be passionately living mine.

The question I began asking myself was, *How do I become more whole?*

To be more complete, peaceful, and harmonious within myself, I'd have to improve my operating system and reduce the internal friction. I'd have to start using the insights and tools to go deeper. I'd have to realize and acknowledge the inconvenient truths keeping me in the chasm I was traveling in. I'd have to deepen my journey of transformation to realize true transcendence. It occurred to me that true wholeness could only be experienced on the other side of true transcendence into a spiritual being.

Being wildly curious and someone always eager to roll up my sleeves and get to work, that's what I did. *What am I willing to try? Anything.* It's a messy process at times. For me, the inconvenience of deep transformation can look something like a five-year-old with watercolors, assorted paintbrushes, and paper. Paint is flying, lots of things are getting painted...sometimes even the paper itself. And in the middle of painting, I might just get up and go outside and ride my bike or just sit and bask in the sunshine. I've been told I'm all over the board when I'm supposed to be focusing. At times this couldn't be more accurate, but in going deep, I try a lot of new things on for size, and my "dressing room" is piled high with stuff that no longer fits me.

WHO AM I?

Who am I? There are so many things that can go into that answer. *Am I the roles I undertake? The masks I wear? Is it genetic, biochemical, or environmental forces that shape who I am? The lunar cycle I was born in? Can I change it, or is it set in stone?*

The answer could be yes to all those and more. Genetics play a role. The combination of biochemicals present when we are born can affect what receptors are most active and what internal chemicals we are more responsive to and seek. Environment can also have a significant effect. That could easily be a whole other book. While understanding causation has its place, when it comes to understanding who I am, its source only matters if it can help me better understand me.

To this point in my adult life, I'd focused on my roles and achievements to define who I am and avoided anything that might expose my core feeling of inadequacy. If I was doing well in my roles and striving for some achievement, that's as good as it got. I fulfilled some of my roles better than others, and I achieved a lot. Unfortunately, my ever-present feelings of inadequacy and lack felt mildly uncomfortable at best and virtually unworkable at worst. I figured if I just kept doing it, it would all work out.

I was the cliche human doing, not spiritual being. Don't get me wrong, that model propelled me to be quite successful in material realms but often left me spiritually bankrupt.

So, who am I? Really.

Self-awareness is an area that I knew I must improve to support my evolution. All too often, I found myself wondering why I did what I did. It was becoming clear that I wasn't as tuned into myself or how I show up quite often as I would have liked to believe. Being more self-aware would give me the tools to better understand how I show up and how the world experiences me. It would help me go deeper into my operating structure and do the required work. It would help me recognize and select the situations that support my strengths and understand and limit those where I am not as effective. I realized that in certain situations, I excelled, and in others, I flailed but often didn't understand why. Ironically, I often found myself in situations and around people I found highly uncomfortable and felt like something was wrong with me.

Not entirely sure of where to start, I decided to revisit personality profiles to better help me understand myself at this point on my journey. My first serious introduction to them came at the Center of Creative Leadership almost twenty years earlier.

In my estimation, personality is the combination of characteristics or qualities that form an individual's human expression. It seemed like some of these tools might help me better understand what was going on with me.

I've thought a lot about the difference between changeable personality traits and those that aren't. My understanding and experience are that we have a core temperament that is much more ingrained than others. It's what more directly affects our behavior. Personally, I think we can change just about anything with full awareness and practice.

When my toxic body, cloudy mind and melancholic emotions were operating with a shaky conceptual framework and operating system, my personality expression was often disagreeable and explosive. My personality is much more grounded and agreeable with a clean body and mind, much more energetic and pleasant emotions, and a simple, authentic, and more transparent conceptual framework and operating system. I have great evidence to show I can greatly influence my personality.

PERSONALITY PROFILES

Personality typing systems aim to provide insight and clarity into one's personality, often through questionnaires. There are many different personality-typing models, ranging from astrological signs to the Myers-Briggs Type Indicator (MTBI) to the DISC profile. These are all human constructs that aim to give some structure and grouping to what seems like an endless number of human personality traits. It's important to remember that all instruments have limitations, and some may be more insightful and easier to understand for you than others. Their roots aren't new, as astrological signs date back some 4,000 years to Babylonian times. Personality traits can reveal things about your behavior that you exhibit consciously and unconsciously. Being aware of your actions and their root will help you realize more of your authentic self. These aren't a cure by any means. They provide insights into who you are and how you show up in this world.

I'd taken a few personality typing tests before and read the results, but nothing about them ever resonated much with me as the curtains on my inner self were tightly shut. With a deep desire to get to know me better and maybe explain some of my behaviors and feelings, this time was different. I jumped in and took a bunch of the questionnaires, studied and compared the results and explored what they might be telling me.

When exploring personality typing, it's also important to remember that we are fluid beings that exhibit behavioral traits on a continuum depending on our state and the situation. For example, in some situations, I may be more extroverted than others, and sometimes my extroversion comes from a place of security and others from nervous tension. Becoming more self-aware has allowed me to better select people and situations that best support me. It's also helped me better understand what I must be on guard for around people and conditions that are more challenging for me.

For example, I am somewhat introverted. If I engage in a highly social event with strangers (a trade show, for instance), I have to consciously work at being social. This isn't a natural place for me, and as a result, I am often exhausted afterward. For me, this means I'll need some downtime to recover. On the other hand, if I am fully engaged in a topic, say self-development and speaking with a small group that I know well, I can fully engage and be energized after the experience. Knowing this about me makes deciding what I do with whom much easier, so I don't end up in situations that exhaust me, wondering, *What's wrong with me?*

I approached personality typing from a descriptive perspective rather than prescriptive. I wasn't looking for them to tell me how to live my life, who I must be or what I must change. I was looking for them to help me better understand what's going on with me.

The astrological model separates personality into twelve groups based on the astrological position of the stars when you are born. I'm a Leo, the lion, and the fifth phase of the cycle. Leo's strengths can be generosity, self-confidence, determination and leadership. Their weaknesses can be naïveté, arrogance, stubbornness and an inability to accept criticism. No doubt, I can see the determination, stubbornness and inability to accept criticism in me.

In terms of the astrological signs, I am more generous, self-confident and determined when I am in an empowered state. For me, an empowered state requires a high level of self-care and self-discipline. When they slip, I slip into the more disempowering traits of arrogance, stubbornness and an inability to accept criticism, mostly because I am already beating myself up.

The Myers-Briggs Type Indicator (MBTI) has sixteen different classifications. I first took the MBTI almost twenty years ago, and while interesting, I didn't understand what to do with it. When I took it recently, I tested as an INTP, the Architect (I for Introverted, N for Intuition, T for Thinking, and P for Perceiving). In 2003, while attending the Center for Creative Leadership, I tested as an ISTP, The Craftsman (S for Sensing).

To give you an indication of the strength of your expression, the MTBI provides a relative score for each category. In 2019, my test indicated introversion and thinking are borderline for me and intuition and perceiving are much stronger. In 2003, Sensing was my most strongly indicated category. Something appears to have changed.

According to my MTBI, my strengths are analytical brilliance, objectivity, imagination and enthusiasm. Being more introverted, much of this occurs in my head, and I can come across as aloof. No argument there. The architect excels at making connections between random pieces of information and relentlessly pursues truth, objectivity and understanding. Often this is not for their own benefit, but they see this as their universal contribution. This book makes more sense now, right? An INTP is enthusiastic about things they are interested in and often playful with people they trust.

My weaknesses, according to the MTBI, are uncertainty, absent-mindedness, condescension, and insensitivity. The architect often lives in fear of failure and worries that they will overlook something. This fits right in with my primary question, *What's wrong with this?* The "absent-minded professor" in me can be scattered and disorganized, and my messy desk would confirm my propensity for this. An INTP can be brutally condescending and insensitive as they push for truth and objectivity. No doubt, I'm often impatient as I am working through an idea and probably come across as way more than insensitive. Quite often, I am so consumed with my latest pursuit I am sure I can seem uninterested in everything and everyone else.

How does this help me? As I continue to be more conscious and present in the moment, I'm able to more clearly see myself and how I show up and often check in with myself. *How can I best contribute in this situation?* is a question I regularly ask myself. With a clearer understanding of how I'm likely to show up in my current situation, I am more likely to be a more empowered version of myself.

The DISC profile separates its typing into four different personality styles, which are Dominance (D), Influence (I), Steadiness (S), and Conscientiousness (C). No style is better than another, and the concept is that we all use each of the four styles but tend toward one style over the other. The DISC profile also provides a ranking on each trait for your natural and adaptive styles. Natural is how you act when you're left to your own devices. Adaptive is how you behave when you feel you are being observed or aware of your behavior.

Dominance type personalities tend to be more confident, demanding and competitive. Influence types are more open, inspired and focused on relationships and influencing others. Steadiness types lean toward dependability and cooperation, and sincerity. Conscientiousness types tend to emphasize competency, expertise and quality.

My scores were; Dominance (49/70), Influence (53/10), Steadiness (69/39) and Conscientiousness (67/53). The first number represents my natural and the second my adaptive score.

The biggest takeaway from this was to see how the DISC instrument predicted my shift from natural to adaptive states. While in my natural style, I am fairly balanced, but when I shift to my adaptive style, Dominance is my strongest trait. Being honest with myself, I become less open, more demanding, and competitive under observation and stress. This works out perfectly in dating. Or not!

How's this help me? With these insights, I prepare for big meetings and social events that will be a more adaptive environment for me. In close relationships, I have to be on guard that I am not unconsciously shifting into my adaptive state as it does not promote connection or intimacy. I need to be tuned into myself so that I am conscious of shifts and manage them instead of letting them run the show.

The Enneagram personality typing system uses nine groups in its model of the human psyche. My first introduction to it was *The Road Back to You* by Ian Morgan Cron and Suzanne Stabile.

Cron suggests in the introduction that you read the book and see if one of the models fits you. He suggests that when you read yours, it may be intense. This idea piqued my interest.

At the time I read this, I had done a lot of work and exploration into myself. Cron and Stabile are very religious and often reference religion. Their view of religion didn't resonate with me at all, but I didn't find the explanation of the Enneagram any less impactful. *Take what you need and leave the rest*, I reminded myself.

In the book, they outlined that "Fours feel something important is missing from their essential makeup. They're not sure what it is, whether it was taken from them or they had it long ago but lost it—only that the missing part is nowhere to be found and they are to blame. The result is that they feel 'different,' ashamed, uncertain about who they are and ill at ease in their world."

They also wrote, "Fours are the most complex of all the types on the Enneagram: what you see is never what you get. There are always more layers of things going on under the surface. Their waters run deep. Who am I? What's my purpose? How does the narrative of my life fit into the grand scheme of things? These are angsty, existential, reading-Albert-Camus-on-a-rainy-day kinds of questions that occupy a Four."

As I read the chapter on Fours, the "Romantics" as Cron labeled them, all the information resonated deeply with me. A Romantic with an Individualistic wing seemed to summarize me better than I ever did. I've also taken several Enneagram typing tests with similar results as my self-classification.

For me, the Enneagram experience was profoundly enlightening and settling. In acknowledging some of my core being and that I wasn't alone in my experience in this world, I found a great deal of peace. It reinforced that I'm not broken nor abnormal. For someone who has often felt ill at ease, this was a complete perspective-changing experience.

An important point to remember is there is no right or wrong personality, none better than the other. When exploring personality typing systems, it's important to be nonjudgmental with yourself and others. It's about better understanding your natural tendency and how you might show up. The work may lead to a better understanding of situations that best fit your unique personality, give you insights into others and how to better interact with them, and insights into why other personality types do what they do in certain situations.

Cron's description of the Enneagram is more of a story, and that resonated with me as well. With that description, I could dig into other assessments and better understand what they might reveal about me. I imagine one typing system or another may resonate better with you and your unique personality, and possibly the composite of a few may give you a better overall view into you.

What was the value of all this for me? Primarily self-awareness. It's like walking into one of those mirror rooms at the carnival, the one where you see every inch of yourself from every angle. They offer understanding in different terms with different groupings, and the composite picture they painted was amazingly clear for me. When I realized that the void I felt and many of the struggles I dealt with my whole life are way more common than I ever imagined, I became much lighter. It opened this gate to a place where I better understand what's going on with me and better embrace who I am and how I may express it to the world. It helped me evolve past letting my personality traits unconsciously run my life and then judging my very core traits as flawed or fighting with them every step of the way. As I evolve into a much deeper state of being, I more often notice my tendencies and adjust when it doesn't align with a healthy version of myself. Understanding me much deeper allows me to not indulge in things that disempower me.

Another great benefit of this work is that as I began to see what other people's types might be and better understand how they might see the world, my view of the world around me became much clearer. In Malcolm Gladwell's book, *Talking to Strangers,* he discusses how our failure to understand each other can lead to harm, especially in the context of some of the significant struggles our culture is grappling with today, such as race and gender bias. It has been profoundly enlightening to better understand myself and how I show up along with others and how they show up. It provides deeper context to the question, *What's really going on here?*

SUCCESS AND FAILURE

I've always hated the word "failure." It evoked a visceral reaction in me. To keep from failing, I even defined the word as not getting up after life knocked me down. Since I always get up, I never fail. One day, I was listening to a motivational talk while working out, and they kept saying you have to embrace failure. *Screw that!* I thought. *You have the word all wrong.*

I leaned into myself and the massive internal friction I felt and began questioning my deep dislike for the word "failure."

Why do I hate the word "failure" so much? and *What must I believe for this to be true?* I pondered.

I looked up the definitions.

> Fail (verb): be unsuccessful in achieving one's goal.

> Succeed (verb): achieve desired aim or result.

> Quit (verb): stop or discontinue.

All pretty straightforward. So, why my strong reaction? Why the friction? Why have I transferred the meaning of quit to fail to avoid failing?

What have I always wanted most since I was a little boy standing at the feet of my dad, looking up to him, both literally and figuratively? Acceptance. The opposite of acceptance? Rejection. The lesson I'd learned as a child was that if you fail at being a son, you get rejected. My young and undeveloped mind connected failure and rejection. With my adoption of a synonymic relationship between rejection and failure, I fabricated a ridiculous story about my relationship with failure.

The story doesn't stop here, of course. To engage in the game of success and failure, I must be able to fail, right? If I can't practically fail, how will I practically succeed? I won't.

Instead, I'll just avoid the game of success and failure. I'll just DO.

Well, then I'll have to not plan and set goals because that will require some form of success and failure. Simple. I'll just leap into the arena and start playing the game like a beast. If I get knocked down, I'll just get up, unbroken.

If I remain unbroken, then I won't fail and won't be rejected. Perfect. No way to get hurt with this elaborately fabricated yet amazingly flimsy story I concocted and lived to the fullest. Unfortunately for me, not so much.

Using this story as my guidepost, I applied it to almost every aspect of my life. Jump in without any definition of success and failure and just do it. I set up a life framework whose outcome looked something like being in the ring with Mike Tyson in his prime, battering at the hands of a heavyweight champ. A graceful entry into the ring with an exit often looking battered, dazed and confused. Without self-awareness of my false, and at times highly disempowering story, I stayed in the ring even at the peril of my existence at times.

As I've stated, many of the events I attended, talks I listened to and books I read discuss having a vision and/or dreams. It's just assumed that you have them. Nope. I don't have a dream. No vision that I could ever reduce to words on paper. I never refined one to be anything close to concrete. Keep it vague, and I can't fail, right? No failures. Don't break. All good. Why confuse things with a vision or a plan? Just be open, jump and grind.

Oh yeah, and to finish my perfectly built house of cards, I also didn't define any boundaries in my life until it seemed to manifest enough internal friction in me that I reacted with some poorly contrived boundaries, which were often met with surprise and resistance from others and the universe.

How have I used this understanding of my past self and past behaviors to evolve?

First, I am very clear on what success and failure mean. To be fully engaged in the area of life, I fully embrace success and failure. I keep success and failure separate from acceptance and rejection, and most importantly, I keep self-acceptance separate from acceptance by others. I focus on that which I can control, accept that which I cannot, and constantly work at improving my ability to recognize the difference.

In terms of daily practice, *What's a win today?* is a regular in my morning journaling prompt. At the end of the day, I'll journal on, *What did I fail at today?* and embrace and relish in being fully engaged in the arena of life, asking, *What lesson did I learn from this?* and *What must I change, or who must I become to not fail at that again?* I almost always include, *What did I do well today?* I love the question *Was I fully engaged in the arena of life today?* and *What did I avoid or escape from today?* Keeping important things at the forefront of my consciousness is critical to my continued ability to be fully present, go even deeper, and live in integrity.

This is one of many examples of my deep dives into truly getting to know and work with me. I've come to realize that internal friction points toward something that I still need to resolve. My journey is to leave no internal friction unclaimed or unresolved as internal friction disrupts my peace, harmony, and freedom. From better understanding the words I use to addressing the friction I feel inside, the journey of evolving our human being and expression is always available.

Next time you find yourself all fired up about something, stop and ask yourself, *What's really going on here?* What keywords do you use? What do they really mean? Why do they have such a charge for you? What meaning have you attached to them? Why?

As I unraveled the fabric of the story I'd elaborately woven, my life became so much clearer. It's as if I turned on a light in a pitch-black room. Now, seeing and understanding the story didn't change anything beyond my awareness. Learning the lesson and applying practices to help me more fully engage and experience life did.

EMOTIONAL AVAILABILITY

In my relationship with my dad, I learned that his acceptance seemed unrelated to my behavior, except that to only be occasionally seen and rarely heard typically minimized rejection. One of the few things it seemed I could control.

Growing up in the '70s and '80s it was pretty clear that boys shouldn't show or discuss emotions. "If you don't stop crying,

I'll smack those tears off your face!" was a popular phrase that didn't get any of the pushback it would today. As someone that naturally feels deeply, this created a lot of internal friction. I felt a lot, but the world was telling me that I shouldn't, and if I did, I definitely shouldn't show it. Like most boys of my era, I learned to hide most of my emotions beyond anger and frustration and had an inner dialogue that reminded me they were wrong.

My experience with my dad and my own inner conflict around emotions helped fuel my lack of self-acceptance and feelings of distrust. I didn't trust myself and didn't trust others, especially when it came to intimate relationships. For the most part, I was emotionally unavailable.

One of the consequences of my lack of self-acceptance was I frequently sought external acceptance. *If the world tells me I'm good, then I'll be good*, my unconscious mind seemed to tell me. In doing this, I let my external world and other people decide how I felt about myself. A framework well suited for a constant supply of anxiety.

Intimate relationships often created conflict for me. With a low level of self-acceptance and trust, I came to a relationship seeking someone else to "complete me." This often resulted in being with partners that also had self-acceptance and trust issues. A recipe for lots of turmoil and drama. And I have a lot of experience with that.

What's self-acceptance? Being able to recognize your intrinsic value as the person you truly are. Being comfortable in your own skin. It seems obvious that you would have to truly know yourself to value who you are.

One of the great benefits of my personal work and journey has been to get to know, better understand, and appreciate my authentic self. This naturally has led me to greater levels of self-acceptance and love. It led me to truly be emotionally available to myself and others.

GRABBING

"Grabbing" is reaching for anything to avoid being fully present with your current situation, especially our current discomfort. At its simplest, it is grabbing for the bag of chips to avoid being with the boredom of a long drive. On a grander scale, it's jumping into a big project to avoid dealing with the failure of a work deal or latching onto a new partner because you are struggling in your current relationship or trying to escape feelings of loneliness. It may be grabbing onto the latest drama or a multigenerational one. It's not the activity that's the issue; it's the avoidance of the lesson that life is offering. To grab is to avoid the opportunity to better understand oneself, learn, and evolve. To avoid leaning into a deeper version of yourself.

To my detriment, I've grabbed onto food, booze, drugs, and relationships to escape and avoid my reality at times to name a few. I may flip that and grab onto a diet, a marathon, or an adventure that is much better for me, but a grab just the same.

At their core, eating, drinking, diets, races, or cars are just things. The reason for my desire is what's important. If I "need" a drink, it's because I want to escape the situation that I find myself in. If I'm running a marathon to run from my reality, it's a grab. If I run the marathon because I love to run and want to test myself, it's not. To repeat, it's not the activity but what's at the root.

When I get overwhelmed, I love to grab big physical projects. My internal world is screaming rejection and inadequacy, so I grab onto a big physical project to divert my internal conflict. It's a way for me to avoid addressing what I need to address. For me, that has often been to escape the acceptance of failure at something.

When I ran from my past, I often made decisions that would "fix" the current situation, not lean into the root cause. Often, they just further complicated my life. I'm getting better at choosing things that better align with me. Often it means taking a deep breath and just being with my current situation for a while. For me, grabbing is often an instant reaction, so I'll let the moment pass before I react. While I'm just being with it, I'll often ask, *What's really going on here?* and be openly curious.

As I started my quest to go deeper into my life, into *me,* I even grabbed for self-help and enlightenment. I consumed books, courses, and ideas. While they have been the fuel that has enlightened my ignorance, at times, they provided shelter from truly going deeper. Jumping from this new idea to that to avoid depth. As I've already said, it's a process.

The transition from grabbing for things to owning my experience sometimes includes some abstinence. This, of course, isn't a new concept. Abstinence has been practiced for a long-time. The key is to embrace the abstinence to go deeper, not as something else to grab onto.

I was inspired a few years ago by a friend to stop drinking for a year, yet I didn't do it immediately. After the holiday season of 2019, I decided to abstain from alcohol for a year. I don't drink often but wanted to experience at least a year without that outlet for avoidance and escape.

For a good portion of my adult life, I said, "I need a drink" after a tough day. This became more routine during the tougher stretches of my life. If I had some success, I said, "Let's have a drink to celebrate." For a year, I abstained from drinking to further lean into truly being me. It wasn't long before COVID-19 dominated the world situation and brought me a number of business and personal challenges that provided excellent opportunities to lean further into my practice.

If I am experiencing a situation that seems to be challenging me, I ask myself, *What's really going on here?*, *What do I need to learn?*, and *What's the root cause of this?* and deeply explore those answers. If I have some success, I truly lean into that as well and embrace what worked well and what the experience is offering me. Building the habit to lean into the situation, cue up the questions, respond to the question, and reward myself with better self-awareness and self-acceptance has paid off way better than the drink ever did. If I do have a drink now, it's to enjoy the drink, not run from my current situation.

The conscious practice of leaning into situations and not grabbing for the ejection seat has been key to my transformation. If I grab, I miss the opportunity to better understand myself and what's going on. If I lean into the situation, I get to experience it fully and maybe even get to its root and learn and apply the lessons I need.

IRRITATION

There have always been people and things in my life, typically on the outskirts, that cause a feeling of irritation in me. I've typically kept them at a distance and told myself a story about their situation that made me feel better. A story that helped me avoid my truth.

For example, I had a friend who was very passionate about women's rights and equality in the workplace. I liked her, yet I regularly felt irritation when I thought about her. I found myself weaving this narrative about how she was "over the top" on this issue and misdirected. Ironically, I fully support that everyone should have an equal opportunity. So, I got curious.

What's really going on here? and *What's this telling me?*

As I explored this more deeply, I came to embrace the reality that my irritation was my deepest desire to be accepted and yet often feeling less-than-accepted. As I previously discussed, I had been focused on external acceptance and not cultivating my own self-acceptance.

My friend's passion irritated my unfulfilled need for self-acceptance, and by asking myself, *What's this really telling me?* and wanting to know the answer, I came to fully understand what it evoked in me, about me.

In manufacturing, engineers often speak of root cause analysis. It's a process for getting to the underlying issue rather than treating the symptoms. Basically, we continue to ask and explore, "What else could be causing this?" until we discover the root cause. The real underlying issue.

Say we are making widgets on a machine, and quickly the widgets are out of specification, off-quality. We ask, "What could be causing this?" We may realize that a bearing in the machine has worn. Replacing the bearing fixes the problem, but the problem quickly returns, and once again, we are producing off-quality widgets, and the bearing is worn. So, we ask again. "What causes the bearing to wear?" We might check the lubrication and find it's not the right one. In this case, it is. What else could be causing the problem? After more questions and exploration, we determine that the machine is vibrating too much. After several more rounds of questions, we determine that the ground under the building was not properly compacted, and the concrete on top of it is flexing with the machine vibration. This is causing the machine to vibrate more, which is causing the bearing to prematurely fail and the widget to go out of spec. The root cause is improperly compacted soil. Unless we resolve that, the problem will persist.

I use this same logic in my personal inquiry. What else could be causing this? What causes that? What's the root cause?

I believe that there is a way for my "machine" to operate in specification (peace, harmony, and freedom) and without vibration (irritation, anger, etc.) once I reconcile the root cause. One guardrail is that I must continually remind myself to embrace what I cannot change, change what I must and know the difference.

If I had learned that the widget machine vibrated too much because the nearby train shook the ground too much, the root cause would be the vibration caused by the train. One could say that the train tracks need to move somewhere else, even though we put the machine in place long after the train was running. In this case, we would look at a system to dampen the vibration from the train to keep the machine stable. It's critical to not spend a bunch of energy focused on the "wrongness" of the train and not get the appropriate dampers in place to isolate the machine from the vibration.

In our manufacturing plant, we have a scale that measures 0.00001 of a gram that sits on a 6,000-pound, two-feet-thick granite table to keep it stable. Sometimes you just have to build enough muscle to dampen the natural vibration of the environment and not focus on the problem that the earth vibrates too much.

In my friend's case, I don't need a 6,000-pound table. I just needed to realize that her passion evoked the opportunity for me to learn a lesson about myself. She is passionate about the right of women to be accepted in the workplace, which provoked my own desire for acceptance. It was another reminder of why my journey of self-realization and transformation is so important. It provided greater insight into an area that I must continue to be better. These days when things like that come up, I lean into the lesson, get to the root cause, and get my "machine" back in spec.

PRESENT MOMENT AWARENESS

Our human journey is impermanent and uncertain. The more we can fully embrace the present moment, the richer our experience.

For most of my life, I've not been present in the moment unless the external situation demanded it. One afternoon a friend was giving me a ride, and he looked up and said, "Wow, the clouds are beautiful today." I thought it was kind of weird and essentially ignored his experience.

His experience got me thinking. Is he crazy or onto something? How does he see that? I almost never see the clouds in the sky when I am driving. Well, he's present in that moment.

Being truly present in the moment allows you to truly enjoy the clouds, stars, moon and sun. It allows you to stop and deeply smell the flowers when they are sitting on the counter or on the trail; I mean actually stop and smell them deeply and just be with the smell. It allows you to be present for yourself, others, and the universe.

In my experience, it's the incessant internal chatter I've facilitated most of my life that kept me from being present in the moment. If I'm always in the past or the future or thinking about this or that, I'm going to be somewhere other than in the moment.

The benefits of embracing impermanence with a quiet mind are many. From smelling the roses on the counter and relaxing during a hot soak listening to some good music are just a few. As I have gotten to know myself better and gotten better at being me, I've learned to stop and smell the roses, look up at the clouds, and truly tune into my current situation.

LIVING TO LEARN

Along my journey, I've evolved from learning to live to living to learn. Learning to live was the necessary triage of me solving a crisis and the looming fifty-four-year-old destiny I wasn't yet prepared for. It was doing the work to stabilize my situation. The truly profound shift came when my journey transcended into living to learn. Fully embracing a journey of personal inquiry and exploration changed everything. It changed how I experience myself and how I experience the universe. Living to learn has become my journey, my reason for being, my meaning. My reason for sharing.

In sharing some of the things that I learned about myself along the way, I hope it helps you on your journey. As my journey transformed into one of living to learn, I've fully embraced the consistent practice of truly getting to know myself better. Truly being better today at authentically being me than I was yesterday.

WHO AM I?

WHEN I TORE OPEN THE CURTAINS ON THE CONCEPTUAL framework that I operated my life with, it was clear that I was unconscious to much of it. I realized that I had no idea where much of it came from, if it was even true, or if I even believed it. Leaning into the situation led me to some pretty deep questions, like *Who am I?*, *What do I believe?*, and *What are my rules for living?*

It led to a lot of exploring, defining, and building a conscious framework that works for me.

In this chapter, I'll lead you through my work in consciously exploring and restructuring my conceptual framework. I'd encourage you to pull out a journal and begin to ask and answer some questions for yourself, some deep questions.

The idea of a conscious framework evolved for me from my emotional work. The idea of recognizing what I feel, being able to label it with words, being able to discuss it and recognize what others might be feeling was a model that had worked well. It occurred to me that doing something similar for the conscious framework might prove useful.

As an entrepreneur, I've often thought about the "elevator speech" that describes my business. From time to time, I've worked on a mission statement, vision statement, company values, and key questions. I'd never done that for myself.

To be honest, I've never been very happy with my company statements. Often, I'd look at other company statements and reword and restructure things I find, but they didn't come from my core belief in my company. It didn't come from my knowing because I didn't know.

As a small company, most days were spent running experiments, producing products, sweeping the floor and putting out the latest fire. Spending much time on the core work of the soul of the company and how it shows up seemed indulgent. It's now clear to me that it is not indulgent for the company, and it's surely not for me and my journey.

A company brand is the whole impact and lasting impression from all that is experienced by the stakeholders, including customers, suppliers, employees, neighbors, and owners of a company. The printed words of elevator speeches, mission statements, and slogans are a guide for the company leaders and a promise to the stakeholders. The brand is the actual experience. In other words, it doesn't matter what you tell me what you stand for or what you are going to do; it's what I experience.

I decided that I need to consciously build my personal operating system with a clear vision on my personal brand and how I, and all the stakeholders of my journey, experience me.

What's my promise to me and all my stakeholders as a spiritual being on a profoundly human journey? I asked myself.

Who are my stakeholders? is another really important question. It's critical to truly know and own your stakeholders. It's equally important not to include those that truly are not.

I was seeking to sort and structure the experiences, learnings, and insights that would form my conceptual framework and personal brand going forward. I was seeking to consciously construct an operating system that's authentically me.

The key to this work is to deeply embrace the distinction between words and experience. The words are great, but the experience is what matters. You have probably been to a restaurant that promises "Great Food, Fast" that served crappy, cold mush and waited way too long for it. The promise is great; the experience sucks! We don't want a brand experience of "Crappy food, served slowly with a bad attitude" but tell ourselves we are "Great Food, Fast!"

Another really important thing I've learned is to not try and be something I'm not or don't believe in. To not buy into some trend or legacy that isn't me. The objective is to paint a picture of the real me and how I strive to exhibit my soul in this universe and own that fully. I would challenge you to do the same. We need more truly authentic souls consciously living their truth, not more unconscious doers, copycats, or failed brand promises.

Realizing the idea of really knowing me and consciously deciding how I express myself in this world was critical to exiting my
chasm, I jumped in. My goal was to paint a deeply authentic
elevator speech of me and define my core conceptual framework
that dictates much of how I function and express in this world.
What follows is what evolved from this work.

I challenge you to start or continue to refine your own conceptual framework and personal brand explicitly.

FIVE WORDS

What five words truly describe me?

Curious (adjective): eager to know or learn something.

Intelligent (adjective): the ability to learn, understand, and
make judgments or have opinions based on reason.

Hard-working (adjective): tending to work with energy and
commitment; diligent.

Adventurous (adjective): willing to take risks or try out new
methods, ideas, or experiences.

Deep (adjective): profound or penetrating in awareness or
understanding.

These aren't just words. These are me and describe me at my
core. They are who I am, not who I want to be or who I want

to project. These words describe me well when you strip away everything around me. For me, these are the words that would describe me in the petitionary, on a deserted island, or in the boardroom. Five words that capture my brand to all the stakeholders, including the most important stakeholder, *me*.

Why five words? No reason on exactly five, except it seemed like enough bandwidth to paint a true picture and not too many as to paint a mural that is too broad and not easily digestible. Five made me refine and get clearer. Yours can be three or ten if that is truly manageable and speaks to you.

After taking all of the personality typing tests, reading a lot and journaling, I decided to take what I needed and leave the rest. I started a daily journaling practice around this idea. *What are the words that best describe me?* is how I started. Like many of my exercises, I didn't allow myself to copy yesterday's work and typically don't read it again for quite a while, if ever. It seems to me, if it comes from my core, it will keep bubbling up. If it's not my truth, it will fade away.

I spent many mornings at the counter writing what came out and often looking up word definitions. *When I say "curious," what does that really mean?*, *How is the word defined, and what's my definition?*, and *Is that really me?* are some of the questions I would ask. Sometimes I would ask myself, *Who am I really?* or *What comes naturally to me?* In conversations with people I respect, I might ask, "Would you consider me a curious person?" to check on my brand experience for them.

For weeks, I just kept up the practice, allotting ten to fifteen minutes each morning. Some words just kept coming up.

Curious was almost always first for me. I'm just curious; it's who I am. I am still the little boy who incessantly asks, "Why?" To kill that would be to kill me.

Intelligence was a harder one for me as it seemed arrogant at first. I love and can sort through things and make sense of them based on reason and data, so I'm intelligent. If the data doesn't fit, I don't accept the conclusion, and that's me. It's who I am, not trying to be.

Hard-working is how I am wired. From the kid who wanted a paper route to wanting to work tobacco fields at fourteen and starting my first body shop at sixteen, I love to work. I've always felt that hard work is the price of admission into the arena. I'm often curious about something and then jump in and want to do the work to understand it and experience it.

Always seeking new methods, ideas, experiences, I'm adventurous. I'm going to jump into something new on a regular basis, or I get bored. That's just who I am. Some may see my brand as "You are all over the board!" and I'm not going to disagree. Curiosity and adventure can definitely be experienced that way.

Deep kept coming up for me. I've got to feel it deeply. If I don't feel it deeply, something is off for me. I'm not interested in superficial or performing for the sake of it. If I find myself, experiences or people being superficial, I feel the internal friction. *I'm not feeling it* or *That just doesn't fit*, I'll say to myself, dismiss it, and often walk away from whatever it is. Along my journey, I've learned that when I go against that feeling, it rarely improves and it often hasn't turned out well for me.

I suggest this practice as a good place to start. What comes up for you? What keeps coming up for you? Is this your intrinsic being, or do you have to try and be this because you think you should? Does it make you uniquely you? Do you truly own it? If I asked someone close to you, would they tell me that's their brand of you?

CORE STRENGTHS

What are my strengths? or *What am I able to do well?* were questions that seemed important to understanding me.

Along my journey, I have seen a number of references to understanding my strengths and cultivating them. The idea is that if I clearly understand the things I do naturally well, then I'll understand my greatest potential and be better able to cultivate and use them. If you were interviewing me, how would I best describe my strengths? If you interacted with me regularly, what would you experience?

I read *Strength Finder 2.0* by Tom Rath a while back and found that interesting, so I went back and took the Gallup Strength Finder Assessment, a psychometric analysis tool. My top five strengths and descriptions were:

1. **Learner:** I have a great desire to learn and seek to continuously improve because I am naturally curious. I love to teach, prefer to read, write and ponder concepts that interest me, thrive in situations that test my talents, and feel at my best when I can channel my energy into things that interest me.

2. **Ideation:** I am fascinated by ideas and can frequently find connections between seemingly disparate ideas. I seek out the unexplored and love to test my limits. Preferring to work alone, I am passionate about finding solutions to complex problems.

3. **Achiever:** I work hard, have a great deal of stamina, and take great satisfaction in being busy and productive. I focus on creating a better future with energy and persistence.

4. **Deliberate:** I take care in making decisions and am very proficient at anticipating obstacles. I select friends and associates carefully as the quality of my relationships is more important than the quantity.

5. **Adaptable:** I like to go with the flow, trust I can handle whatever happens, and fully accept life's uncertainty.

My top five strengths seemed to describe me well. One thing I really liked about the instrument was it provided a solid way of organizing and describing my strengths in actionable ways. Once again, I kept focused on the top five because that's manageable for me. You may want a few more or less. Nothing magical in five.

Once I had identified my strengths, I worked on writing a short narrative about each of them that resonated well with me. It's not just a word, but how the word truly describes me from my core being. I'll refer to these from time to time to help me better clarify what I can bring to my situation or why I'm struggling with an activity that might be way out of my strengths.

Whether you take an assessment or do the work on your own, start developing a short list of what you do naturally well as they are your areas of greatest potential. It may help you better understand yourself and provide some clarity on areas to focus.

BELIEFS

What do I really believe?

As I got deeper into truly getting to know myself, I realized that I wasn't at all clear on what I believe or why I believe what I do. Especially the beliefs that define my arena of being.

On the surface, that sounds a bit strange even to me, but it's true. I didn't know what or why I believe with any real certainty. In other words, I couldn't coherently and precisely articulate the things that I believe that make up the core of my being. Like a lot of things on my journey, I was convinced I knew, but when pen came to paper, it was something less than wholesome.

It occurred to me that if I don't know what I believe, then I'm operating my entire life unconsciously on a bunch of random beliefs. A bunch of beliefs that might not even be true for me. Considering how much time and energy I put into this life, that seems ludicrous. Doesn't it?

What do I really believe? and *Is that really true for me?* were questions that kept coming up.

As the technique had proven quite effective in other areas of my transformation, I decided to start working on this and for months journaled on the question *What do I truly believe?* Again, I didn't look at yesterday or copy past versions. I just let myself write them. For beliefs, I didn't limit the number because these are my operating manual and to limit them would leave blind spots unexamined.

For months, I answered the questions *What do I believe?, Why?, Is that really true?,* and *Are these consistent with my brand experience?* These must come from within, as this is the foundation of how I show up for myself and the universe. This is how I operate my life; they are not cute slogans or something for me to put in this book to impress you. These are my working definitions of me. They evolve with me as my journey, lessons, and work help forge them to be sharper.

With each new journal, I rewrite and revisit my beliefs. It's a time to reflect on the lessons of my journey during my last journal and check in with myself and my beliefs. It's an opportunity to sharpen and refine them for even better peace, harmony, and wholeness.

Take the time to do this work! And be patient and honest with yourself. This may not come easily. It may surprise you. I surely surprised me. Do you believe this and execute your life by these? Would you defend this belief? Is this your experience with yourself? If I knew you and read this, would this be my brand experience of you? They nor you will always be perfect, but they will be your truth if done authentically. Your guidepost for your operating framework.

Below is a snapshot of my beliefs while writing this book. For the most part, they are in no particular order beyond the first few.

1.   Purpose: The purpose of my life is to consistently live more fully as a spiritual being having an extraordinary human journey. To be better at being me today than I was yesterday.

2.   **Responsibility:** I am completely responsible for my human experience. My life is my responsibility and my responsibility only. I own 100 percent of my entire journey and am not a victim. It is no one else's responsibility except mine to live fully and be a better me each and every day.

3.   **Integrity:** Above all else, I must be in integrity with myself and with the universe in being honest and strong. I must know and trust myself, know my rules, and conduct myself in accordance with them. When I do not, I must own it fully and amend it.

4.   **Becoming:** It's not what I get, how I look, where I go, or who I know. It's who I become in the process. Becoming is mine to keep; the rest is just passing by.

5.   **Appreciation:** I appreciate all of the amazing journey of my life as it's presented to me and strive to be fully present in each moment. The fact that I am here and awake is an extraordinary gift.

6. **Acceptance:** I fully accept the things I cannot change, change the things I can, and know and practice the difference.

7. **Uncertainty:** Truth is, I will know what's going to happen when it happens and what people will do when they do it. Expecting anything more certain is futile.

8. **Impermanence:** I passionately embrace the impermanence of life. Life doesn't come with guarantees except that it is perfectly impermeant. In accepting this, I am able to be present, appreciate, and fully experience this moment.

9. **Surrender:** Many things are presented to me in the flow of my journey. They are here for a reason, and I embrace the offering. Quite often, it's not obvious in the moment, but it is striking how the dots can be connected looking back.

10. **Conscious:** I strive to be fully aware of what's really going on in each moment; otherwise, I'm running me unsupervised.

11. **Body:** I respect my body and nourish my ecosystem. Living fully requires me to be in total harmony with my body.

12. **Lessons:** My life journey is a series of lessons that I must embrace, learn, and apply. If I pass on the lesson, I will continue to repeat the experience until I learn and apply it.

13. **Practice:** A life well lived requires an absolute commitment to a vibrant daily practice that grows with me and is practiced regularly. It is my responsibility to do the work, consistently realign, and be better at being me today than I was yesterday. It's a long game, not a sprint or a show.

14. **Work:** Hard work is the price of admission to living fully. Working hard, sometimes beyond exhaustion, is the price of having fully lived. It is not punishment. It's a privilege and absolutely necessary.

15. **Grit:** Embrace discomfort, suffering, and even extreme discomfort. It is required to live fully. It's not always about finding an easy way and definitely not about escape; it's about rolling up my sleeves and staying with it, even in the perfect storms.

16. **Emotional Agility:** I embrace all my emotions and consistently work at better understanding what they are telling me. I am not a victim of them, nor do I let them run my show. I passionately dance with them.

17. **Grabbing:** If I am grabbing, I am trying to escape something that needs my attention, and I must seek to understand what I am attempting to avoid or escape. It's not to beat myself up but to lean in, embrace, understand, and be better.

18. **Question:** I question everything and always strive to ask even better questions. The quality of my life is in direct proportion to the quality of the questions I'm asking myself.

19. **Relax, rest, and unwind:** While fully embracing my journey requires hard work and some discomfort, it also requires perfect rest and recovery time. It is required to remain in harmony with myself.

20. **Jump:** Only those who risk going too far can possibly find out how far one can go, and more often than not, I wildly underestimate just how capable I truly am.

21. **Simplify:** To solve things, I must frame them in the simplest and most solvable form possible. If it seems complicated, it's likely I've complicated it to mask my fear and avoid jumping in.

22. **Reality:** What seems to be going on here is often not what's really going on here. Take the time to better understand the situation and root cause of the condition.

RULES

So, how do I take all this work and live a better life?

Knowledge is the theoretical or practical understanding of a subject. Application is the action of putting something into effect. Experience is an event or occurrence that leaves an impression. Rules are a set of principles governing conduct.

To truly live an authentic life, we must effectively execute the space between knowledge, application, and experience. Knowing something and consistently applying true knowledge is where the benefits and authenticity are realized. Rules are the tool that governs our conduct in the space.

What rules do I live by? is the question I asked myself.

Like many things I uncovered along my journey, my answer was less than clear or compelling. All too often, I said I believed one thing and did something else. The very definition of hypocrisy.

What's the opposite of hypocrisy? Integrity.

If I want to be in integrity, then I must show up in a manner consistent with what I believe and know to be true. My authentic self. My truth. Rules are my guides in this space.

No doubt, we are all living by a set of rules whether we are conscious of them or not. For me, many of my rules were unconscious, erratic, inconsistent with what I said I believed and at times wildly disempowering. A challenging framework and perfect recipe for consistent internal and external conflict and distress.

To truly achieve internal peace, we must minimize internal conflict. Having a clear set of rules that are aligned with our beliefs builds a conscious framework well suited to deliver lasting internal peace.

I decided that I needed to be clear on the rules that I operate within. My set of conscious principles that govern my conduct, that I aim to live by. A short list that guides me in making decisions from moment to moment. These define how I show up. How I take what I know and believe and apply them to my human experience. They guide me to deliver on my brand promise.

A clear set of rules is especially important in more difficult situations. When there are conflicting situations or issues, rules help cut through all the clutter. If we are feeling stressed, rules help guide us. If your number one rule in battle is "no man left behind," that guides one set of behaviors; if it's "each man for himself," that guides another.

I like to write these on an index card, and I have it in my wallet. In the eye of a personal storm, I might pull them out to remind myself how I am committed to showing up regardless of the situation. It's my contract with myself.

I didn't limit the number of rules but continue to work at keeping it as compact and manageable as possible. I've found too long just isn't executable, and too short leaves me without the guides I need. You need as many or as few rules as needed to be authentically you.

Here is the list that currently resides handwritten on an index card in my wallet. With each new journal, I rewrite a new card and sharpen and refine them. I also have them as a note on my phone.

1. Do what's right because it's right.

2. Be better today than yesterday.

3. Trust your knowing.

4. Be present.

5. Appreciate.

6. Focus. Work. Finish.

7. Keep it simple. Don't complicate.

8. Accept what is. Change what you can. Realize the difference.

9. Do what you can, with what you have, where you are.

10. Feel it fully. Understand it. Then let it go.

11. Think Deeply. Question often. Seek to understand.

12. Seek, learn, and apply the lessons.

13. Respect others.

14. Inspire by example.

15. Breathe!

The benefit of having a conscious set of rules is they provide the framework for my decisions and actions. If I know my rules and consistently apply them in my life, I am more likely to be and do what I believe. I am more likely to deliver my brand promise. As I work and refine them, I can see what's working and what's not.

As I move through my day, I often refer to rule number one, "Do what's right because it's right." If I am struggling with a decision, I will run down my rules and see if my plan meets my rules.

My rules evolve as I do. From time to time, I write them in my journal and sharpen and refine them as needed. I ask myself, *How am I doing?*, *Are my rules helping me deliver on my brand promise?*, and *Are my rules helping me be better at authentically being me?*

What are your rules? Are you living them?

How about an index card or a digital note on your phone? How about sharing them with someone you trust?

STUMBLING BLOCKS

"What causes me difficulty?" can be a very empowering question for me.

While focusing on the empowering facets of my being, I find it's also important to know and look out for the things that have and can cause me difficulty. These are the things most likely to trip me up and that disempower me. The things that serve up "cold mush" in my brand experience.

While I have done a lot of personal work and transcended into a spiritual being, my old ways still linger in the bushes, ready to pounce. It's taken me some work to acknowledge and fully accept this. Early in my transformation, I realized old patterns would sneak in and highjack me from time to time. This often left me feeling disappointed in myself and wondering what was going on.

Our current neurological understanding of our brains in very simplistic terms is that the old wiring never gets removed. It's ours to keep, forever. The new habits we form create a new and sometimes more dominant pathway in our brains, but our old, dysfunctional "path" is still there, hard-wired. It turns out that our brains are a lot like the internet. Once the picture that we wish we never posted is out there, it's in the digital space for good.

Why is this important? We need to keep an eye out for those disempowering things that are lurking in the bushes waiting to sabotage our present moment. We need to be aware of them and get back on the highway when we find that we veered off onto the old disempowering path again.

This is one of the most profound learnings for me along my journey of transformation. I always have to be on the lookout and dance with the things that sabotaged me before. There is nothing broken or wrong with me. I didn't fail. In these moments, I acknowledge what's going on and correct. It's a dance. And the more we own our dance, our truth, the more authentic our journey. The goal is not to be perfect; it's to be perfectly you and better today than we were yesterday.

What are traits that can derail you? Start your own list and own it proudly. Embrace the power in owning all of you and building the muscle to dance with it all. Owning your "bumps" means not letting them define you consciously or unconsciously. Not blaming it on *That's just the way I am.* Being brutally honest and owning your inconvenient truths lets you quickly recognize them and self-correct, which is a success to be super proud of. Here are some of mine, my reframe, and some questions to help me to a more empowering state of being that I embrace at the first sign of any of these.

	DISEMPOWERING TRAIT	EMPOWERING STATE
Acceptance	For as long as I remember, I have wanted to be accepted. For much of my life, I have chased this or that and given away my power to others in search of validation.	I am whole, fully accept myself, and completely own my journey. Who am I, and what do I believe and live?
Envy	Often, everyone else seems to have it easier, have more friends and better relation-ships, make more money, or live a more beautiful life.	I am a spiritual being on my own beautiful human journey. My hope is that everyone lives their own amazing life. My journey is my journey. What do I truly appreciate? What's going well?
Grabbing	I've grabbed for things to escape my internal discomfort and friction. From an early age, it's been food, alcohol, drugs, sex, work, drama, and on and on.	I've got this! Leaning into the discomfort leads to better truth, and that is where I must go. What's really going on here? What am I feeling? What lesson do I need to learn and apply?
Victim	My default pattern was to be the victim, sometimes of things that hadn't even happened.	I own me and my journey. I accept the things I cannot change, change the things that I can, and fully embrace the difference. How can I more fully embrace my truth?
Complication	To mask my fear, I've built a complicated story that became unsolvable, and *voila*, I move into victim mode.	I keep it simple and solvable. If it's not solvable, I simplify. If it's still not solvable, I try again. If it's still not solvable, then I accept that it's just a situation. How can I reframe this into simple and solvable?

MY ELEVATOR SPEECH

So, who am I? While it's interesting and necessary to explore, I needed a compact description of myself. I needed a way to tell the story of me and my brand experience for myself and the universe. To lay out my soul, my conscious framework, and reflect the growth I'd done throughout my work. Clarity improves integrity, so my elevator speech helps me remain in integrity with myself.

Take some time to craft your own elevator speech as a way to comprehensively understand your framework, make a bench-mark for yourself, and your own evolution. You must be clear on who you are and how you show up to truly own yourself and your journey.

Here's today's version of my ever-evolving self.

I am a spiritual being on a beautiful human journey. Being inspired, I'm fully engaged in the arena of life and consistently seek to be more fully alive and deeply realize me. I am passionately curious, artistic, and intelligent and was born to build. I embrace hard work, as I believe it to be the price of admission into the arena and definitely required to bridge life's chasms. A critical thinker, I am most motivated in creating something new and typically find routine tasks much less interesting and often quite challenging. It's my curiosity that gets me started, but sometimes I struggle to finish as my interest wanders elsewhere. I am laid back with an even temperament yet have no issue taking charge if it interests me. If I am truly interested, I want to understand it, experience it, and genuinely feel it.

I'm totally open to new ideas, highly flexible and adaptable, don't need a plan, and thrive in the midst of seeming chaos. I may even create it from time to time to keep routine things interesting. I can be aloof in nature; I develop relationships selectively, only when I feel a true, deep connection with another person. I'm content alone and often need space to think and recharge. I like to live my life and let you live yours. I'm not looking for anyone to save me, don't expect help, and gladly accept full responsibility for attaining what I want as I know my biggest barriers are most often self-imposed.

Adventurous at my core, I courageously jump into the deep end that shows promise, as I believe only those who risk going too far will ever know how far one can go. As a gleeful rebellion, I am likely to dismiss the tried and true, typically find structure stifling, and am not opposed to ignoring the rules, especially if they interfere with my curiosity. I don't mean any disrespect, but this is my journey, and I am going to experience it on my terms. No doubt I've gone too far and paid the price at times, but I continue to push today's impossible as I know it often becomes tomorrow's reality. While I've grabbed onto many things to avoid and escape truth, I continue to evolve and work toward fully embracing my convenient and inconvenient truths. I integrate practices into my life that feed my soul and align my human expression so that I continue to thrive and evolve. My goal is to be better at being me today than I was yesterday. I am whole, genuinely enjoying my journey, and hope I can inspire others to do so as well.

My elevator speech is a "living" construct of me. It evolves for me as I get better at being me. At times, I use it to check in with myself in relation to how I am being and how I am showing up for the universe.

Sometimes I read it for fun. Sometimes to remind me of my commitment to myself. From time to time, I share it with people who I know will give me honest feedback on their brand experience of me.

Want to practice your vulnerability? Hand your elevator speech to someone who you know will give you honest feedback. Ask them to give you brutally honest feedback on how well your elevator speech and their brand experience of you align. Then truly listen to what they tell you.

With each new journal, I write the latest version of my elevator speech on the first few pages. Then I truly ask myself and honestly answer, *How am I really doing?* and *How can I be better?*

CONSCIOUS FRAMEWORK

Knowing who I am, my strengths, what I believe, my rules, my stumbling blocks, and my elevator speech and consciously working them has profoundly improved me and my journey. It's my conscious framework. It's the framework that allows me to better deliver my brand promise to myself and to all my stakeholders. It guides me in being more whole today than I was yesterday. It's been pivotal in helping me transcend from an unconscious and often suffering human doing into a spiritual being truly enjoying an extraordinary human journey.

16

THE ART OF BEING FULLY ALIVE

"The sculpture is already complete within the marble block, before I start my work. It is already there. I just have to chisel away the superfluous material."

—Michelangelo

Like Michelangelo's works, we all have glorious sculptures within. Life's real work lies in chiseling away our superfluous material to reveal our truth and freedom. Much, if not all, of the superfluous stuff are the cages we wandered into and allowed ourselves to be confined by along the way. The prisons that keep our truth and freedom locked away deep inside us. For all of us, if we do what is easy, we'll keep our truth and freedom locked away, and our lives will be less fulfilling and ultimately more difficult. If we do what is hard and break out of our self-imposed confinement, our lives will be easier, and our journey, far more rewarding. No one can do our work for us. No one is coming to save us. There is just no way around the inconvenience of this truth.

The disconnected and randomly acquired conceptual framework that defined my life was covered in the curtain of my unconsciousness. That curtain was ripped open at my dark, dead-end. I knew I would have to chisel a lot of superfluous material to even get a glimpse of my authentic self. To be perfectly honest, I had no idea what, or how long, it would take. It took courage to leap into that unknown space and even more courage to stay with it when the rubble was piling up at my feet, but I couldn't even see an outline of a sculpture yet. Fortunately, once I got immersed in the depth of transformation, closing the curtain and returning to unconsciousness was no longer an option.

My calling to write this book and its original title were early in my quest for self-discovery and self-realization. At the time, I felt directed to write a book, yet I wasn't entirely sure about what or why. I'd never written much and surely didn't feel qualified to write a book about much of anything deep. While I had lots of experiences and insights, it's a whole other thing to write a coherent book that's worthy of anyone's time and attention.

"Calling" and "direction" are mediocre descriptions of what I felt. In the midst of the absolute chaos of transformation, I was being told to write a book from deep within, deep beyond me. The power was undeniable, and the feeling was as clear as anything had ever been in my life. When I speak of surrendering and embracing life's journey, this is a great example. Any rational self-evaluation would have concluded that writing a book at that point in my life was a ridiculous idea for me and discarded the notion of it. The calling wasn't my ego; it was the universe.

As I struggled with writing this book, the parallels to my personal journey began to emerge. The book was chaotic, as was my transformational journey. There were lots of good nuggets, but nothing that felt like a cohesive story. They both felt like all the parts were scattered all over the floor, weren't labeled, and didn't come with an instructional manual. It was clear that I had some work to do on both my personal and book fronts. First, I needed to do my own work before I could present it to the universe. In truth, writing this book has been an amazingly effective catalyst for my own transformation. It was like writing my own instruction manual while I worked to put it all together.

The original title, *Moving My Mountain*, was exactly where I was. I was running from the suffering and chaos that all too often dominated me and moving what felt like a mountain that held me back from a rich, deep life. My fuel was fear, plain and simple. That title was *it*, and if you asked, I would have told you there was no way it would ever change. My mindset at the time was that I was never going to get "there," and at best, I would always be moving my rocks of discontent.

At times, the chaos and struggles of transformation felt like my own personal Pandora's Box. It felt like I had opened my "box" and unleashed a flood of "hidden" facets of my being that truly needed attention, many that I didn't like one bit. I used my past struggles, my crash, the legacy of generational suicide, heartbreaks, and a truly dark dead-end to remind me how bad things can get. I used the gauntlet of fifty-four to drive me even when there was no sculpture in sight. It inspired me to work relentlessly even when I was exhausted from it all. It was a massively uncomfortable experience at times. Many times.

If this is at all familiar to you on your journey, let me offer you hope and encouragement. There is a glorious sculpture within you. It's there in all of us. At times the storm may seem like it's more than you can bear; it was often that way for me. You are stronger than you realize, and this storm, too, will pass. If you consistently chisel away at the superfluous stuff and truly keep getting better at being you, your experience will get better too. One day, you'll realize *the* storm has passed, and you are standing on the morning after, watching a sunrise you never imagined.

As I continued to study, learn, and adopt the lessons, my journey evolved from one focused on what felt like a monumental task of chiseling away the boulders of superfluous material to one more focused on the beautiful sculpture that lies within me. My journey was transcending from the work of "moving my mountain" to something deeper, lighter, and more inspired. It felt like I was breathing life into my soul and had given myself permission to live from it.

I began to truly realize this transformation a few years after my dark night, well into my exploration and deep work. Way, way later than I had anticipated. I gradually realized that I wasn't focused on all the stuff that needed to be removed but began to see and feel me. I imagine it's similar when the artist starts to see the sculpture emerge from the giant block of stone.

On your journey, this may take some time. The euphoria of starting the process of self-realization and transformation may have long worn off. At times, you may feel like nothing seems to be working, like the whole thing is pointless and going nowhere. Keep working! A glorious sculpture is there, no doubt. It is in all of us. If what you are doing isn't working, try something else. Try a lot of something else's.

The first book I wrote went to the digital graveyard. Maybe it was a publishable book, but it didn't inspire me. It was like a long list of stuff that I had been exposed to rather than a journey of real transformation. A long list of pieces and parts with little insight into how to put it all together because I hadn't figured out how to take what I need and leave the rest. Once I began being more alive, it no longer spoke to me. As I transcended further into being my soul, I could feel a real shift in everything about my life. Moving my mountain represented tearing down the old conceptual framework and entering the unknown of forming a new one. A more authentic and truer one.

It was 22° on a chilly morning when my son and I pulled out of the driveway. "Isn't life amazing? It's twenty-two outside, and here we sit in a climate-controlled car with heated seats, the sky is clear, and the sun is shining bright, the stereo sounds amazing with music beaming down from satellites in space, and my digital assistant will answer just about anything I ask from the world's information."

He looked at me and said, "Wow, aren't you in a great place?" in a slightly sarcastic tone of a teenager.

"Yes, I am!" I said genuinely. It surprised me about as much as it did him.

The phase of my life, my old title *Moving My Mountain*, faded, and for a time, I felt like a book without a title. "Coming Soon" describes it well. I embraced the uncertainty of it all, something that hadn't come easily to me earlier in life. For the most part, I'd stopped trying to manipulate the world to deliver me fulfillment and make me feel okay. I knew that what I needed would present itself when I was ready for it, when I truly earned it. In my daily journaling, I pondered, wandered, and looked up the definitions of many words. I've learned to just write and explore, not push things that aren't ready to reveal themselves yet.

On your journey, this may feel unsettling, to say the least. You may have done a lot of chiseling and feel like there is no sculpture in there. Stick with it; it's all part of the journey.

As I drifted along without a title, I felt a growing sense of something. One day on a call with Su, she said, "It sounds like you feel alive."

That immediately resonated. "That's it; I feel alive," I replied. It's a deep sense of aliveness, not an adrenaline-fueled event. No transaction. Not an accomplishment. A growing trust in myself and a confidence in simply being me was emerging. It's being still and peaceful. It's being free. It's as if the internal storm has gone away, and I was standing on the morning after experiencing the amazing sky at sunrise.

Over the next few days, I looked up words and explored.

Art (noun): the expression or application of human creative skill, knowledge, and imagination.

Being (noun): the nature or essence of a person.

Fully (adverb): to the fullest extent.

Alive (adjective): full of energy and spirit.

The Art of Being Fully Alive (noun): The expression and application of human creative skill, knowledge and imagination to facilitate the true essence of a person to the fullest extent of their soul, energy, and spirit. It's the beautiful process of continuing to realize the sculpture of our soul that lies within us all.

That describes my philosophy on being a spiritual being on an extraordinary human journey.

The art of being fully alive characterizes my journey on the other side of the space that separated the often suffering, human frantically doing, trying to manipulate the world to deliver him fulfillment, and the spiritual being. What it didn't describe was the massively inconvenient truth of the deep and sometimes dark space that separated the two for me.

One day I looked up the definition of the word "chasm."

Chasm (noun): a profound difference between two situations.

In the world of personnel development, "gap" is often used to describe the space between where you are and where you want to be. "Gap" doesn't come close to describing the difference between the unconscious and often suffering me and spiritual being.

"Chasm" spoke of the deep exploration and work of real transformation. It spoke of the profound space that separates the two situations. The years, the struggles, the sweat, the tears, and the intense work.

The beauty of "chasm" is its meaning evolves as I do. It's a deeply serious word that conveys the depth of life's journey and the responsibility of self-realization and spiritual being. "Chasm" evokes the challenges and utter chaos of real transformation, practicing the art of being fully alive and the beauty of transcendence in me.

That begins to tell you why *Chasm* is the title of this book.

What happens on the journey of crossing life's ultimate chasm toward realizing true transcendence into spiritual being? While tearing down the flimsy conceptual framework that no longer serves? While chiseling the superfluous stuff that covers the potential of a fully realized soul? For me, the most profound thing is that I've become an artist of my own life. I am constantly getting better at the expression and application of human creative skill, knowledge, and imagination to be better at simply being more authentically me. More peaceful, better harmony, and more freedom. More whole.

After more than fifty years of struggling with the real essence of my life, that ever-present void that irritated and often tormented me, drove me, and was sometimes my closest and only companion, I came to the other side of the chasm of self-realization and transcended from running after the next thing that was going to "complete" me into simply practicing the art of being fully alive.

While I am in a profoundly better place of being, life is still offering me plenty of difficult lessons and storms. I am still a single parent of a teenager, run a small but demanding company, occasionally dating, and consistently seeking better health. The storms still come and go, and I seem to get better with each new one. My life is amazingly rich, and I truly appreciate all that I get to be and do. While living fully isn't always easy and is nothing like I thought it would be, it's so much better than I ever imagined.

I've often wondered and tried to find an explanation of the difference between soul and spirit that resonated with me. As I wrote this book, I realized what they mean to me. My soul is my core being, the fundamental definition of who I truly am, my unique definition as a body of energy. It's the "book" of me that I read.

My spirit is the expression of me. It's my soul, body, mind, and emotions. It's the whole of my *being*. It's the book the universe experiences. It's my brand expression.

Along your journey of transformation, you'll start to see glimmers of light and realize more and more moments where the tools you're chiseling with don't feel so awkward. As you become better and better at truly being you, there will be times when you genuinely feel like you are the artist of your own glorious sculpture. Truly appreciate these moments; you deserve them. There will be moments when the tools seem less effective. Lean into these too. It's really hard work at times, but I can promise you, nothing feels better than realizing you are truly the artist of your own being and journey. Nothing feels better than realizing more and more of the glorious sculpture that lies within you. When you realize the art of being fully alive has become your journey. It will most likely be the most rewarding thing you ever experience.

PLANTING SEEDS

FROM THE ONSET OF THIS BOOK, I'VE BEEN COACHED TO WRITE to a specific audience or, even better, a specific person. After scrapping my first book, I decided to write to my younger self. The seventeen-year-old naïve teenager who threw his cap high up in the air at high-school graduation with the journey of a lifetime ahead and absolutely no idea what was to come.

What do I wish I had known then? I asked myself.

As I looked back on my journey so far, I was looking for those things that have made a difference in my life: the things that worked and those I was ignorant to but were revealed on my quest of self-discovery, self-realization, and transformation. I wanted to plant the seeds in my young mind so that they might sprout in the right season of my journey.

As a parent, I've often wished I could transfer all my life lessons onto my child to save him some of the struggle, but if you are anything like me, you realize they have to live and learn their own lessons. Maybe some of my insights will be helpful when life's storms roll through his life as well.

Wherever you are on your journey, my hope is these words will resonate with you and aid and inspire you in crossing your chasm, now or in the right season of your journey.

BE BETTER AT BEING YOU TODAY THAN YOU WERE YESTERDAY

"The unexamined life is not worth living."

—Socrates

Who am I?, *What do I really need?*, and *What will I contribute?* are questions that I never really thought about. Looking back on my life, I was often so busy searching for something to fill a void I couldn't define that I never stopped to learn about myself. I was too busy doing to allow myself to get to know and be me.

A mindset of being a better version of being you today than you were yesterday may be the greatest gift you will ever give yourself. It's the greatest gift I ever gave myself. When I lost my expectations and embraced the appreciation of me and my journey of self-discovery, my entire being shifted. When I embraced the consistent practice of going deeper, chiseling the glorious sculpture that lies within, and practicing the art of being fully alive, my human journey as a spiritual being bloomed, and I realized what I had always been seeking. Peace, harmony, and freedom. Truly appreciating and being me.

Learn what you need to thrive. Strive to live it, be it. Know what you believe and continue to refine it along your journey. Be conscious about your rules and strive to live in the highest level of integrity possible. Truly feel, embrace, and understand your emotions, but don't let them run your show. Develop your personal elevator speech and let it be a living document. Let the world know who you are because that's how the universe experiences you, not what you tell us.

If you ever catch yourself saying, "That's just the way I am," remember that what you are saying is, "I don't like the way I am behaving either, but I am not sure what to do about it, yet."

Truly realize that today is an opportunity to be better than you were yesterday.

As Viktor Frankl said, "Between stimulus and response there is a space. In that space is our power to choose our response. In our response lies our growth and our freedom."

DO WHAT YOU CAN, WITH WHAT YOU HAVE, WHERE YOU ARE

Don't wait for the stars to align or the world to change to fully be yourself and live your authentic life. Be a better version of yourself today than you were yesterday, no matter what situation you find yourself in today. Start right now, where you, with what you have. Don't waste an ounce of energy or a minute waiting or complaining about what you don't have or what's not right. Don't wait for tomorrow.

If you live to be seventy-two, you have about 38 million minutes in your body on this planet. It seems foolish to squander any of them focused on what you don't have or waiting for the right one to come along to truly live. Treat each minute as if it were a hundred-dollar bill and spend them well. You're going to spend the next hundred, and the next, and the next whether you like it or not, so you should get the best return on your spending. Besides, we have no idea how many "hundreds" are in our bank.

Do what you can, with what you have, where you are.

APPRECIATION

"What's wrong is always available, so is what's right!"

—Tony Robbins

The first step in creating a fulfilling life journey is to recognize and deeply embrace this truth. Even in the perfect storm, there is a valuable lesson, an opportunity to contribute, an opening.

To appreciate is to recognize the full worth.

In every moment, there is a reason to live fully, appreciate, and contribute.

What can I truly appreciate in this moment? is one of the most powerful questions I know. It changed the very foundation of me and my journey.

JUMP IN, EMBRACE YOUR JOURNEY, AND LEARN AND APPLY THE LESSONS

A big reason for where I am is that I have been curious and embraced what life offers, especially the faint and subtle opportunities along the way—school, work, relationships, adventures, this book, etc. I'm who I am because I was open to the subtle cracks and faint whispers that had no promise of outcomes, just experience. The experience is the gift, not the outcome.

If there is one thing that I am even more aware of today, it's the faint whispers and subtle opportunities. They are presented for a reason. For a needed lesson, not a desired outcome. They probably won't take you where you think, but if you fully embrace them and do the often-hard work, they will provide the lessons you need.

What lesson do I need to learn and apply? is a foundational question to graduating the current class on life you find yourself in and a prerequisite to truly continuing your journey.

Don't wait for someone to invite you; walk through the open gate, push it open, or jump over it if you must.

As Abraham Lincoln said, "Things may come to those who wait, but only the things left by those who hustle."

RESPONSIBILITY, DISCIPLINE, AND DAILY PRACTICE

Like a young plant, you have roots and the expression the world experiences. The roots are your responsibility and your responsibility alone. Focus on growing strong roots and consistently and persistently being better than you were yesterday. Growing beyond your roots may look great in the moment, but the first big storm will shatter your facade.

A young plant needs constant nourishment, as do you. You must feed your body, mind, emotions, and soul to flourish. If you starve your plant, it wilts and may die. I've learned that it's the hard work you put in behind the scenes that builds the roots of your being, so feed your body, mind, emotions, and soul things that nourish deep root growth. Pay special attention to things that help you flourish and those that cause you to wilt.

Use what you have available at the moment, and don't waste any energy on the distraction of what you don't have. Be brutally honest about finding the root causes. Be courageous in changing the things that you can and accepting the things you cannot. It's often not what you think it is. No matter what your life serves up, strong roots can weather even the perfect storm.

Commit time every day to train your body, mind, and emotions and be better today than you were yesterday. Don't fool yourself; there have always been twenty-four hours in a day. You must train yourself each and every day.

SURRENDER, CONTROL, AND WISDOM

"God, grant me the serenity to accept the things I cannot change, the courage to change the things that I can, and the wisdom to know the difference."

—Reinhold Niebuhr

Your journey will be a dance between the flow of those things you can control and those you cannot. The gift is to truly understand and practice the difference. Spend as much of your time and energy on things you can control, and don't waste any on those you can't. One clue to look out for is if what you want requires someone or something else to change, move on to something you can control. It's a much better investment of your time and energy.

CONTRIBUTION, COMPETENCE, AND GIFTS

Always ask yourself, *What can I contribute?* rather than *What can I get?*

Contribution raises our universal energy and, ultimately, your own. Neediness drains the universe and ultimately leaves us all hungry. Contribution need not be grand. It may simply be working hard at your vocation and being a model for others. It's often seemingly small acts, such as taking the time to listen to someone who needs to be heard, that make the world a better place.

Competence is the ability to do something successfully and efficiently. At your core, always strive to be more competent at being and expressing yourself. As it relates to your vocation, choose something that aligns with your being and be consistent and diligent at improving your competence in it each and every day. To this day, when I pick up a mop and mop the floor, which I do fairly often, I do it with total integrity as I believe how I do anything is how I do everything. Nothing is below me or above me.

I believe we all have inherent gifts. If you know what they are, nourish and treat them as the most meaningful things you'll ever be given. If you haven't revealed them, keep exploring and remain ever open to their revelation. Always be open to realizing new gifts.

SUCCESS, FAILURE, AND POSSIBILITY

Success is simply the accomplishment of an aim or purpose and failure, the lack of it. To succeed on your own terms, you must have an aim or purpose. When used properly in the areas you can control, success and failure are merely instruments to allow you feedback on whether your skill, strategy, and execution are efficient and effective at producing your desired aim or purpose. Failure just means you haven't succeeded, *yet*.

Remember that your journey is uniquely your journey. Comparison is useful in terms of your progress on your journey. It's a giant waste of energy to compare your journey to others' journeys to evaluate your success or failure. You aren't walking their path, and they aren't walking yours. What you can control is your journey. If you compare yourself to others, do it to see what's possible, not judge yourself. Focus on being better on being you today than you were at being you yesterday. Compare you of today to you of any yesterday and where you are on your journey today. Appreciate your progress.

GRIT AND GRAB

Grit is courage and resolve in the face of resistance, especially fierce resistance. Grab is to grasp for something to relieve your obligation to lean into the lesson life is presenting. If I'm grabbing for something, then I'm not developing my grit or learning my lesson.

Grit is a muscle, and you must develop and continue to develop the muscles of courage, resolve and persistence in the face of resistance to realize it. Like any other muscle, grit fades with lack of exercise and needs consistent training. Regardless of where you are on your life journey, grit is required if you are going to lean into life and truly practice the art of being fully alive. Without developing strong grit muscles, I fear your life will be so much less than your potential.

Developing grit requires that you lean it into struggle, some-times intentional struggle. Running those miles when your body is saying no, pushing out another rep when it seems impossible or grinding on that project when all you want to do is go take a nap. Train grit daily, and when the storm comes, you'll truly appreciate the strong roots you've developed.

Grabbing is to "punch out" on life's flight. Once it gets uncom-fortable, we seem almost wired to grab the lever and eject. This takes many forms, including avoidance, escape, and quitting. As with much of life, taking the immediately easier path, like "punching out," will rarely lead to being better or experiencing a better life.

IMPERMANENCE

Impermanence is one of life's truths. Nothing is permanent. I've found that the better I embrace this truth, the better my being and my journey.

Impermanence is the reason to be fully present in each moment because once they pass, they are gone forever. The "hundred" has been exchanged for the experience of that moment. Impermanence assures that tomorrow will be different from today, and life provides no guarantee we'll experience tomorrow anyways.

Impermanence makes hanging onto the illusion of control a waste of the current moment and energy.

Building the muscle of fully leaning into the moment and embracing it regardless of what it presents is crucial to mastering the art of being fully alive and fully living your truth.

OWN YOU AND YOUR JOURNEY

Don't spend an ounce of energy or a moment of time being a victim. Own you and own your journey. Life has never been easy. Life has never been fair. It never will be. I spent many minutes and considerable energy stuck in the futility of victimhood whining about how this or that was unfair. It's never improved the situation, me, or my being a bit. It has made the situation less agreeable for sure.

Navigating your chasm and realizing your potential so that you can master the art of being fully alive requires total ownership of you and your journey. It doesn't come with a *Get Out of Jail Free* card. It requires a brutally honest assessment of your situation, hard work, appreciation, and grit. It's all within your domain of control and divine potential as a being. It's a foundational root in realizing your full potential and wholeness.

QUESTIONS AND TRUTH

Just because you believe it doesn't mean it's true!

Much of what you already believe is untrue. That's right; it's completely false. It's a lie you picked up somewhere along the way and continue to feed.

Questions are the antidote to disempowering and often false beliefs. The quality of the questions you consistently ask yourself will be directly related to the quality of your being and experience. To your wholeness.

While life may seem ridiculously difficult at times, there is a path in your domain of control that leads to a better you and a better journey. Great questions and your real desire to know the answer will be a key tool in helping you navigate.

Always be clear regarding what you believe and consistently test your beliefs against universal truths.

THE ART OF BEING FULLY ALIVE

In some of the harshest places on earth, I have realized a being so much better than I imagined possible. In some of the most beautiful places, I have so massively under-realized my potential and completely missed the beauty of the moment; it's embarrassing to admit.

Being fully alive is to embrace oneness. We are all connected. Everything is connected. It's all part of the universal ecosystem.

To be fully alive, we must realize that we are an integral piece of it all. Billions of years lead to this moment; billions more will lead to another. Oneness is the universal truth that everything is connected, has been and always will be.

May you master the Art of Being Fully Alive for yourself by passionately embracing your full responsibility as a spiritual being on your own uniquely glorious human journey. If you live this fully, when you take your last breath, you will have known triumph and defeat and be one of the courageous souls that dared to fully remain in the universal arena of being.

PUTTING A BOW ON IT

IT'S BEEN QUITE A JOURNEY SO FAR. FROM THE LITTLE GUY beaming a soul smile at three years old to the awakened soul writing this, life has presented me and continues to present its share of lessons. I've teetered on the edge more than once, and at times, the gravity of the situation seemed like it might be more than I could bear. Thankfully, it wasn't.

Along the way, there have been many amazing moments, experiences, and love that contributed to the richness. There has been tragedy, loss and some brutally harsh lessons as well. For a long stretch, my journey just didn't seem to make much sense, but something inside wouldn't let me settle for *That's just the way I am* or *That's just the way it is.*

On that dark night, my existential crisis delivered me to a place of no return. It opened the gate of my self-imposed prison, and I began my quest to enlighten my ignorance as to what was going on. With more openings and awareness, I became immersed in self-discovery and self-realization. As I began to integrate the things that truly spoke to me, I began to free myself from negotiating with the universe to deliver me fulfillment and settle into naturally being. As even more of my truth was revealed and I truly integrated and opened even further, I came to a tipping point and awakened to my soul. I transcended from negotiating with the universe to knowing and living my truth. I transcended from learning to live to living to learn, truly being better today than I was yesterday and passionately practicing the art of being fully alive. I began to truly realize my wholeness.

That place of peace, harmony, and freedom I was seeking, the one I always knew deep inside me was possible, is no place at all. It's the journey. It's consistently being more deeply me. More deeply connected. More deeply whole. Peace, harmony, and freedom flourish when my whole being is collaborating, mutually supportive, and mutually beneficial in sync with our soul. It's that simple. It's rarely easy. It's worth it. It's our responsibility.

It turns out that the very point of our human experience is to consistently chisel away the superfluous stuff and reveal ever more of the authentic and beautiful sculpture that is our soul and limitless potential on our terms. To consistently cross our chasms, practice the art of being fully alive and contribute to the wholeness of our universe in our own unique way. To free ourselves from our ignorance and self-imposed limitations. To free ourselves from our own prison. To actually be free.

To truly embrace our chasms, we must accept that our past, present, and future situations, do not define our being. Wherever we come from, whatever we have or haven't done, this moment is an opportunity to go deeper and live more authentically. To freely choose our response.

We cannot wait for life to be easy to be whole. We must do what we can, with what we have, where we are. Wholeness appears to have no limits, and life—well, it's rarely easy.

It seems to me that the very meaning of life is to become ever more whole and leave the world a better place than when we were thrown into it.

If my next breadth were my last, my human body would come to rest aligned with my soul. I have crossed my chasm and transcended from a frantic human doing to an awakened soul deeply living his human experience on his own terms. It's my life's most important and rewarding work. It's the work I believe we were all meant to do and share.

May you fully experience your journey and reveal the beautiful sculpture that lies within you. Venture deeply into your chasm, practice the art of being fully alive and embrace all that it offers. Jump in, especially when it terrifies you, because only by risking going too far will you know your true limits. Passionately embrace the hard work because it's the price of entry into the arena. Do what's right because it's right. Feel it all and allow yourself to truly see and be seen. Think deeply and challenge your thoughts and feelings. Appreciate the depth of the sky above and the vibration from the ground below. Love like you won't get hurt; embrace it when you do. Smell the glorious scent of the flowers, really listen to the symphony of life and deeply appreciate the touch of our soul. Embrace the joy and the pain.

Get up, dust yourself off and keep fighting. Dance in the pouring rain, cry till you laugh, and laugh till you cry. May you weather the perfect storms with utmost integrity, learn, and apply all the lessons and leave the gate open for others. May you truly experience peace, harmony, and freedom.

May you always be better at being you today than you were yesterday.

—ME. ♥

Epilogue

WAKING UP
FROM MY CHASM

July 26, 2020.

Iт's EARLY MORNING, AND I AM SITTING IN MY CHAIR ALL ALONE on top of the world. It's my fifty-fifth birthday and my "wake up" from my 365-day sentence of living in the shadow of generational suicide. I came to Thunder Ridge on the Blue Ridge Parkway in Tennessee this morning because it's where I was called. As the sun is rising in the east, I am on the other side of the mountain looking west. A part of me wants to see the sun crest the horizon, one of my favorite things, but I am where I am supposed to be. The sunrise looking west is more expansive, deeper. The colors flow in broad strokes across the awakening sky. There is a beautiful elegance in this view. Wholeness.

Just maybe, looking west foreshadows that day when I will take a last breath and how I now live to truly enjoy the beauty, peace, harmony, and wholeness of my being and my journey. How my chasm no longer represents a void but a beautiful opportunity to continue to embrace, experience, and evolve. A journey in consistently being even more authentically me.

I came to this spot prepared with my journal and pen to write the closing of this book. Having no expectation and knowing that whatever was meant to be would be, and I would write it. This is what my soul had to say...

MY JOURNEY...

To know the beauty of my soul.

Feel it.

Live it.

Be one with it.

To feel my body and the swirl of the cool breeze over my skin.

To see and truly love the view.

Endless beauty.

Limitless possibility.

To hear the flow of the trees.

The song of the birds.

The smell of beauty.

The vibration of the earth.

The symphony of life.

The connection of our soul.

To love my life.

To love ME.

To Be Fully Alive.

Welcome Home, Bob.

AUTHOR'S NOTE: IN HONOR

OVER THE THIRTY-FIVE YEARS SINCE THE CRASH, I HAD ALWAYS felt the deep uneasiness about surviving it, about being the perpetrator and lone survivor. At times, I wondered why I was spared and would do anything to undo what I did, but, of course, I cannot. Frequently I wondered how much of life I dare enjoy, or if I deserve any peace and enjoyment at all?

In counseling and coaching, I was asked on multiple occasions, "What if you forgive yourself?" and I've always said and meant, "I am not looking for forgiveness; I don't think it's even fair to ask for it."

Through my work, I learned to accept what I did because I did it. My insanely reckless behavior caused two people's human journeys to end that night. It was my fault, no one else's. I never meant to harm anyone, but I caused a horrible tragedy and immense suffering.

The day at DWD, when I shared my past, I unconsciously knew I had to become transparent and own my whole journey, so I shared my story and have so in this book.

May this book and my work honor you both. May the energy that was extinguished not be wasted. May it be a source of hope and transformation for others. May it give something back for all that I stole. May my work respect you both and inspire other lost souls to find their way home more quickly and spare the universe more needless tragedy.

With my deepest respect and honor.

HOLDING THE GATE OPEN

ALONG MY JOURNEY, I'VE LEARNED AND BEEN AIDED BY MANY. My experience is that crossing life's ultimate chasm requires inspiration, knowledge, and sharing. Once we pass through a gate that others have held open for us, it's our responsibility to hold it open for others in our own unique way. Authentically sharing our journey is crucial to helping our collective soul evolve.

Thank you to everyone who has been and will be part of my journey. I deeply appreciate you all!

There are a few people that truly stand out so far. People that held the gate open for me to go deeper.

Stew Berman, PPC, CLC, CMC: From our first call more than a decade ago, you were the mentor that helped me begin the process of self-discovery, self-realization, and transformation from a human frantically doing to a spiritual being deeply experiencing a beautiful human journey. Thank you for all the time you held the gate open and allowed me the opportunity to realize a new level of learning and evolution.

Paul Whetnall: Of all the people who have graced my life, you have always impressed with the breadth that you see the world in. Your insights into how others might see the situation have profoundly helped me develop better insights and responses. Thank you for all the hours you have spent with me working the long list of situations I have found myself in while building my company. You are my role model in unselfishly holding the gate open for others.

Dr. Randy Wall: When you said, "How will you know when we are done?" during our first session, the insights that followed opened a huge gate for me. Eager to transcend from the darkness that had tormented me for most of my life, your insights, and guidance helped me truly begin my transformation. Thank you for being there when I needed someone to hold the light up for me to see.

Su Thomas: Along the journey of transformation, you appeared when I was ready to truly transcend into spiritual being. Virtually every time we talk, you grace me with an insight to frame the things I am experiencing and feeling. Sometimes it's the words; sometimes, it's the entire experience. Thank you for opening the gate and walking next to me on my spiritual journey. You have been a guide in the depth of being, never judged, and often helped me understand what I was experiencing. I will forever be grateful for your guidance.

Tony Robbins: From an infomercial that set a seed to an intervention at DWD in 2017, you and your work have been a beacon of light out of my darkness. When I raised my hand, and you said, "What's your name and where you from?" to the hug we shared later, you provided a space for me to step out into the light. In that moment, I did something that I'd resolved I would never do and broke the chains that I didn't even know were holding me back. Without you and all the peak experiences I shared with you, my journey would look much different, and this book—well, it probably wouldn't be.

David Deida, Christopher Sunyata, and John Wineland: Your insights, experiences, and practices helped me transcend deeper into spiritual being. At a crossroad in my journey, I was able to go deeper and realized that my journey had just begun. That, in fact, it was the journey, not the destination. With your example, my practice continues to deepen and evolve. Thank you for sharing your depth and insights.

Manjit: At the small wooden table in the courtyard of the Mother Teresa's Missionaries of Charity House in Varanasi, you held the gate open and invited me to transcend into spiritual being, spiritual wealth. There is barely a day that I don't feel you saying, "and I have everything I need." The energy we shared is part of my soul and constantly reminds me that our deepest contribution comes from the wealth of our soul, not our material world. That in a simple moment, we can so deeply share and contribute to the wealth of our oneness. I will always carry you with me and hold the gate open for others as you did for me.